how to play Poker

hamlyn

Poker

how to play

and other gambling card games

Peter Arnold

First published in 2003 by Hamlyn, a division of Octopus
Publishing Group Ltd
2-4 Heron Quays, London E14 4JP

Distributed in the United States and Canada by
Sterling Publishing Co., Inc.
387 Park Avenue South
New York, NY 10016-8810

ISBN 0 600 60922 7

A CIP catalogue record for this book is
available from the British Library.

Card designs based on Waddingtons
No. 1 Playing Cards

WADDINGTONS NO. 1 PLAYING CARDS
© 2003 Hasbro International Inc.
Used with kind permission of Hasbro

Publisher's Note
Throughout the book individual players have been referred
to as 'he'. This is simply for convenience and in no way
reflects an opinion that poker if a male-only game.

Printed and bound in Italy

10 9 8 7 6 5 4 3 2

CONTENTS

INTRODUCTION

Poker, in all its forms, such as Draw and Stud Poker and their variations as well as Texas Hold 'Em and Omaha, is nowadays one of the most popular card games both in casinos and at home.

origins

Poker was invented in America. It did not spring into existence fully formed, but took its main elements from a number of earlier games, the most notable of which was Bouillotte, a nineteenth-century French game which had itself evolved from an earlier game called Brelan. In Bouillotte, four players were each dealt a three-card hand from a 20-card pack (A, K, Q, 9, 8 in four suits), and the thirteenth card was turned face up as a common card that all the players could use to improve their hands. The players would bet on their hands in a similar way to today's poker players, the hands being ranked simply as four of a kind, three of a kind or two of a kind. The highest hand won the pot, and four or three of a kind with or without the up-card won bonus chips from the other players.

Dead Man's Hand

One of Poker's best-known legends is that of Wild Bill Hickock, who made the mistake of playing poker in a gambling saloon in Deadwood in 1876. For once he didn't take a seat with his back to the wall. A gambler called Jackie 'Crooked Nose' McCall, who had been hired by other crooked gamblers to kill Hickock because they feared he might be made marshal of Deadwood and clean up the game, walked in and shot Wild Bill in the back of the head with a Colt 45. Bill died clutching his hand, which was found to be two Aces and two 8s (some say all black), with the odd card either the Queen or Jack of diamonds. From that day, pairs of Aces and 8s have been known as 'Dead Man's Hand'.

Another game often mentioned as an ancestor of poker is a Persian game called As-Nas, which was played with special packs of 20 or 25 cards according to whether four of five people were playing. Each player received five cards and, again, they bet as in poker. The winning hand was the one with most cards of the same rank.

The French game Poque was played in a similar way to Bouillotte and As-Nas and is probably the origin of the name, poker, especially as the first references to poker place the game as being played around New Orleans, in what until 1803, when Napoleon Bonaparte sold it to the USA for $15 million, was French territory.

development

From 1836 references to poker by name appear in books. At that time it was played with a 20-card pack (A, K, Q, J, 10 in each suit) and four players were dealt five cards each. Hands were ranked, from highest to lowest – four of a kind, a full (i.e. A, K, Q, J, 10), three of a kind, two pairs and one pair. The top hand (four Aces) was an outright winner, unlike a royal flush in modern poker, which can be equalled. In fact, in the old form of the game a full was unbeatable, although it could be equalled, because it precluded an opponent holding four of a kind. This form was known as Flat Poker.

It was not long before poker was being played with the full pack of 52 cards. By 1850 this form had completely overtaken the 20-card game, and was briefly known as Bluff. With 52 cards the flush was recognized as a distinctive hand, and the straight, the full house and the straight flush were later also given recognition. Strangely the straight was not at first universally given its proper place in the ranking order, as some players thought that three of a kind should outrank it.

variations

The use of the 52-card pack allowed players to improve their hands by changing some cards if they wanted, and the draw became a standard part of the game, and this version of the game became known as Draw Poker. By 1865 an American 'Hoyle' mentioned Stud Poker, supposedly a game started by cowboys in Ohio, Indiana and Illinois. Spit Poker, Jackpost Poker, Whiskey Poker and several other variations of the game were soon being played. The sheer variety of poker games has made it difficult for 'official' rules to be drawn up.

social climbing

If poker itself developed rapidly over 40 years or so of the mid-nineteenth century, so did its place in society. It had begun in the early days of the nineteenth century in gambling saloons and was associated widely with card-sharps, cheats, gangsters and anybody else out to make a quick buck – the Mississippi riverboats became notorious as places where passengers were fleeced by professional gamblers. By the end of the century poker was more widely played as a respectable and entertaining private game, played in homes among friends and acquaintances.

Nowadays casinos and clubs are again important places to play, and some high-stake casino games played by experts receive wide publicity and are closely followed in the press. Since the mid-1980s a 'World Series of Poker' has been televised in the USA and in 1999 such a poker game was arranged and televised over several days by Britain's Channel 4 and proved very successful, being followed by further series. Poker, in its history of 200 years or so, has never been so popular.

---

quote

INNOCENT: 'Poker'? Is that the game where one receives five cards? And if there's two alike that's pretty good, and if there's three alike that's much better?'

HUSTLER: 'Oh – you'll learn the game in no time.'

W.C. FIELDS, Never Give a Sucker An Even Break.

How to use this book

CHIPS

- Stakes and antes are represented by circles; the numbers in the circles represent the number of chips.

- White chips indicate those staked in previous betting rounds.

- Grey chips indicate those staked during the current betting round.

- Orange chips indicate those in a side-pot in Stud Poker.

CARDS shown face up but shaded represent cards in the players' hands or face down on the table.

PLAYERS coloured orange represent those no longer in the hand.

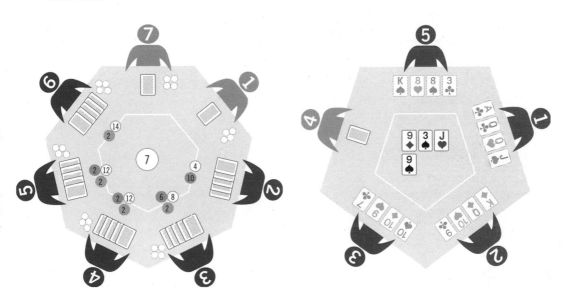

INTRODUCING POKER

the object of poker

The object of the game is to win money or the *chips* representing money, from the other players. This is achieved in a succession of *deals* which last either until an agreed time, until all the players remaining in the game agree to stop or until only one player remains, all the others having lost their stake money. Each deal is complete in itself and is not affected by previous or subsequent deals.

Each player in each deal is dealt a poker hand of five card; in some games, e.g. Seven-card Stud Poker, each player selects his five-card hand from a larger number of cards. In successive rounds of betting, each player bets that he holds a better poker hand than any other player. Players place their bets towards the centre of the table, the accumulated bets becoming the *pot*. A player may fold (pull out of a deal) at any time, but loses any stakes he has already bet in that deal.

A deal finishes when either all players but one fold, and he takes the pot, or a *showdown* is reached. The remaining players reveal their hands, and the player with the best hand takes the pot.

At the showdown, if two players or more have equally good winning hands the pot is divided between them.

Most poker games can be played in a 'High-Low' version, in which the player with the best hand, and the player with the 'worst', share the pot. In some versions, one player can win 'high' and 'low' with the same hand.

the general rules of the game

Poker continues to evolve, and has resisted attempts to impose universally recognized laws upon it. As early as the nineteenth century at least one code was drafted, but this was mainly to prevent cheating. Many clubs and casinos have their own rules and many books have been published setting out general practices.

This section relates to practices common to all forms of poker. How to play specific versions of the game follow in the parts on Draw Poker and Stud Poker, etc.

the number of players

The number of players in a poker game can vary from two to fourteen, depending on which version is being played. Players may join a game that has already started, so it is usual at the start of a game to agree a maximum number. Draw Poker is best played with no more than seven players, and Stud Poker with no more than ten. When the maximum number of people is playing, no one else can join until one of the current players leaves. Players can decide at the beginning of a game not to admit latecomers.

the cards

The standard pack of 52 cards is used, with the cards ranking:

A (high), K, Q, J, 10, 9, 8, 7, 6, 5, 4, 3, 2.

The Ace can also be used at the end of the sequence 5, 4, 3, 2, A, where it is ranked low (see page 12). It can't be used in the middle of a sequence, e.g., 2, A, K, Q, J.

The suits are equal and not ranked.

wild cards

By mutual agreement, any card or cards in the pack may be designated wild. The holder of a wild card may use it to represent any card he wishes, except that in some schools he cannot use it to duplicate a card he already holds, i.e. if he holds all four Aces, his wild card cannot represent a fifth Ace. If a player has a pair of Kings and a pair of 4s, he can use a wild card to convert his two pairs to a full house, which ranks higher. Equally, if he has three of a kind, he can use a wild card to improve it to four of a kind.

Originally, the most common way to introduce a wild card to poker was to use the Joker as a wild card in a 53-card pack, but now it is more usual to specify one whole rank as wild, most commonly the 2s (deuces). The black deuces are usually used if only two wild cards are wanted.

More on the use of wild cards appears on page 34, including which combinations most schools do not allow, how they affect the probabilities of certain card combinations appearing and how to value hands when wild cards are used. In the descriptions of games in this book, wild cards are not used unless stated.

ranking of poker hands

The ranking of poker hands is shown below. From highest to lowest they are as follows, with the first number quoted being the number of such hands possible in a 52-card pack without wild cards being used, the second figure showing the probability of being dealt such a hand straight from the pack, and the third the probability expressed as a percentage.

TABLE 1: The ranking of poker hands

		Combinations	Probability	Description
1st Straight flush		40	1 in 64,974 0.0015%	Five cards of the same suit in sequence. Between two or more straight flushes, that with the highest-ranking top card wins. A tie is possible.
2nd Four of a kind		624	1 in 4,165 0.00240%	Four cards of the same rank, with an odd fifth card. Between two similar hands, that with the higher-ranking four cards wins. There cannot be a tie, so the fifth card is of no consequence.
3rd Full house		3,744	1 in 694 0.1441%	Three cards of one rank (i.e. a *triple*) with two of another (i.e. a *pair*). Between two full houses, the one with the higher-ranking set of three wins. A tie is impossible.
4th Flush		5,108	1 in 509 0.1967%	Five cards of the same suit, but not in sequence. Between flushes, the one containing the highest card wins, if equal the second highest, and so on. Ties are possible.
5th Straight		10,200	1 in 255 0.3925%	Five cards in sequence, but not of the same suit. Between straights, the one containing the highest card at the top of the sequence wins. Note that A, K, Q, J, 10 therefore beats 5, 4, 3, 2, A, where the Ace counts low. Ties are possible.

- *The cards in a flush are exactly the same value as each other, e.g. the hands are tied.*

  ♥10, 8, 7, 6, 3   ♣10, 8, 7, 6, 3

  In this situation the pot is split between the two players.

- *The cards of the two pairs are exactly the same, e.g.*

  ♥K, ♦K, ♣7, ♠7   ♠K, ♣K, ♦7, ♥7

  The fifth card determines the outcome. If this is also the same, the pot is split.

		Combinations	Probability	Description
6th Three of		54,912	1 in 47 2.1129%	Three cards of the same rank with two unmatching cards. Between similar hands, that with the highest-ranking three wins. Ties are impossible.
7th Two pairs		123,552	1 in 21 4.7539%	Two cards of one rank, two of another and an odd card. Between similar hands, that with the highest-ranking pair wins, if equal the highest-ranking second pair, if equal the odd card. Ties are possible.
8th One pair		1,098,240	1 in 2.3665 42.2569%	Two cards of one rank with three other unmatching cards. Between similar hands, the highest-ranking pair wins, if equal the highest-ranking odd card, if equal the next highest ranking, and so on. Ties are possible.
9th Nothing		1,302,540	1 in 1.9953 50.1177%	This hand lacks an accepted name, and is sometimes called a 'no-pair' hand or a 'high-card' hand. Hands of this type are ranked by the highest-ranked card they contain, if equal by the second card and so on. Ties are possible.

chips

In a casino or club, where everything is supplied, from table to cards, the game will be played with chips. Usually there are four denominations, denoted by white chips, red chips, blue chips and yellow chips. The value in cash of a unit is variable – some tables having higher stakes and being more 'valuable' than others. In private games cash may be used as stakes, but it is preferable to play with chips. The players determine in advance the value of each colour in units, and the value of the unit in cash before anyone buys his chips. For example, a white chip worth one unit could represent anything between a penny and a pound in Britain, or anything from a cent to a dollar or a euro, etc. elsewhere. In this book, in each example of specimen games, we will describe the betting in terms of chips only.

COMMON CHIP VALUES

white	red	blue	yellow
1	2	5	10
1	5	10	25
1	5	25	100

banker

If chips are being used, the players should select one player to act as banker, who has first choice of seat. He has charge of all the chips and issues them to the players, including himself, at their cash value, and redeems for the appropriate amount the chips of players who leave the game.

jargon-buster

wild card a card which by prior agreement its holder can use as any card he wishes.

chips tokens used in poker instead of money.

pot the total of the stakes which have been bet, and which the winner takes.

triple, trey or trip three cards of the same rank.

pair two cards of the same rank.

burned card a discard from the top of the pack.

time limit

Before play begins, players should agree on a time at which play will end. If other players join the game later they are bound by the time limit. Players are free to leave the game earlier if they wish.

seating

After the banker has chosen his seat, other players may choose seats if they wish. If there is a dispute, the cards are shuffled by any agreed player, and cut by another. The banker then deals a face-up card to all of the other players. The player dealt the highest card (Ace high) has first choice of seat, the next highest card the next choice, and so on. If two players draw equal cards, they are dealt a second card to break the tie.

changing seats

Players can change seats at any time after one hour of continuous play, and again at any time after another hour of play. If a player wants to change seats and someone else disagrees, repeat the seat-choosing process.

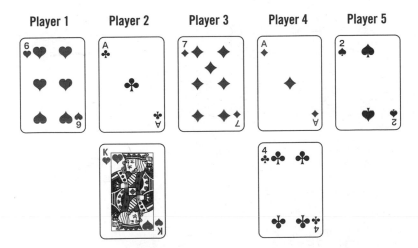

CHOOSING SEATS Players 2 and 4 were both given Aces in the first deal, and in the second deal player 2's King beats player 4's four, so player 2 may choose where to sit first, followed by players 4, 3, 1 and 5 in that order.

the sequence of play

In poker, everything passes to the left. The dealer deals the cards, clockwise, one at a time to all the players, beginning with the players to his left, the turn to bet passes from player to player to the left and when each hand is over, the player to the left of the previous dealer deals.

first dealer

Once everybody is seated, the first dealer is chosen in the same way as seats are chosen, except the banker this time deals a card to himself as well as the other players. If two players or more hold equal highest cards the banker deals a second card to each of them. The player with the highest card is first dealer.

In a casino, where the dealer is not one of the players, a button or disc is used to designate the player who would otherwise be the dealer, and this button passes round the table to determine who receives cards first, who bets first, etc. This is a simple way of avoiding arguments about who's turn it is.

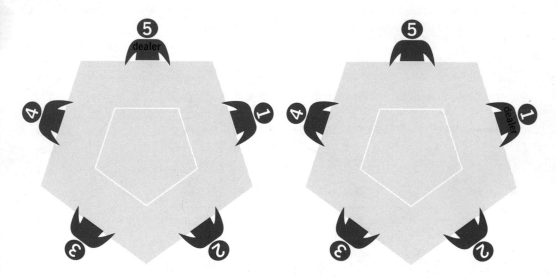

PROGRESSION OF THE DEAL AND PLAY The person to the left of the dealer is, in most circumstances, the first person to receive cards and to bet. When a hand is completed, the deal and turn to play first move to the left.

antes

To make the game more rewarding, financially, in most forms of poker a number of chips are put into the middle of the table to start the pot before each deal. These are called the *ante*. Most commonly, each player puts one chip into the pot before the deal. For convenience, sometimes the dealer puts in for all players, e.g. if there are eight players, the dealer puts in eight chips. After eight deals, each player's contribution in antes is equal. The ante is placed in the centre of the table and usually, for convenience, kept separate from the stakes each player bets during the deal, as the amount of each player's bet should be easy to see. The winner takes the ante and the bets at the end of each deal.

BIG AND SMALL BLINDS

Sometimes, instead of an ante, where all players put in, a blind bet is made by each of the first two players to the dealer's left. The first player puts in one chip called an ante, or small blind. The second player puts in a larger amount, agreed beforehand, say two chips, called a straddle, or big blind. The third player is the first to bet voluntarily. The small and big blinds are placed in front of the players making them, since they count as actual bets rather than antes.

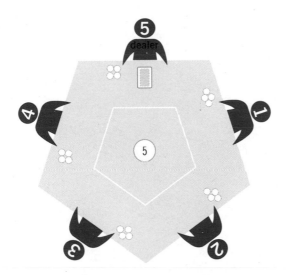

ANTES AND BLIND BETS In the ante, each player will contribute an equal amount, say one chip, to a pile in the middle of the table, as shown. Where only some players contribute, as in the system of big and small blinds, the chips count as part of the players' bets.

shuffling

Before each deal, the cards must be shuffled at least three times.
Any player may ask to shuffle, but the dealer shuffles last.

1 Hold the pack face down in the fingers of your left hand, with your left thumb holding the pack on top. With your right hand grasp the majority of the cards from the bottom of the pack.

2 With your left thumb, pull off six to12 cards from the top of the pack while your right hand takes the main part of the pack over them. The cards in your left hand drop into your palm.

3 Bring the pack over with your right hand, slip a few more cards off with your left thumb and repeat the process.

cutting

After shuffling, the dealer then places the cards before the player to his right, who cuts by removing some cards from the top of the pack, placing them on the table and putting the remainder of the cards on top of them. Both parts of the pack during the cut should contain at least five cards.

If the player to dealer's right declines to cut, the obligation passes to the player to his right. The only reason to refuse to cut is superstition. If all the players refuse to cut, the dealer should do so himself.

1 Lift a proportion of the cards off the top of the deck, without looking at the bottom card or allowing anyone else to see it.

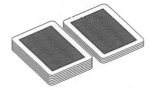

2 Place the removed cards next to the pack.

3 Put the main part of the pack on top of them.

dealing

After the shuffle and cut, the dealer *burns* the top card of the pack by placing it face down on the table to begin what will become a pile of discarded cards as the game progresses. He then deals the cards one at a time to each player, including himself, beginning with the player to his left. The number of cards dealt, and whether they are face up or face down, depends upon the form of poker being played.

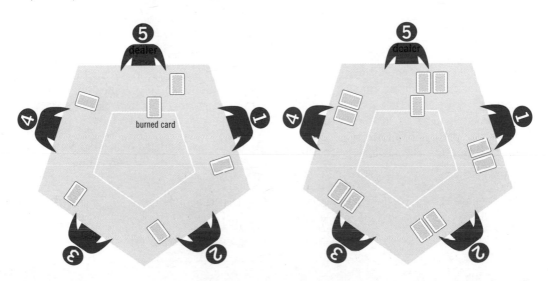

betting

In all forms of poker betting takes place during what are known as *betting intervals*. In each betting interval, one of the players has the right, or the obligation, to bet first. Each player thereafter in turn is required to do one of four things (a fifth option, to check, which applies in certain circumstances, is mentioned later, see page 24):

BET

A player opens the betting by placing a number of chips into the pot, announcing the number of chips he is betting. He might say, 'I bet two.'

CALL

A following player puts enough chips into the pot to make his contribution to it equal to the highest better so far, but no higher. He retains his interest in the pot. He announces he is calling, and the number of chips he is putting in. He might say, 'I call for two.'

jargon-buster

betting interval a period in the game when the players have been dealt some or all of their cards and in which they bet, call, raise, fold or check. The number of betting intervals varies with the form of poker being played.

betting round during a betting interval, a betting round ends when all players have had an opportunity to bet once. The first player to bet then has the option to bet again, and a second betting round begins. Successive rounds take place until all bets are equal, when the betting interval ends.

bet to place stakes into the pot.

call to place stakes into the pot to equalize the total stake with that of the previous better.

raise to place into the pot enough stakes to equal the previous better, and to add more.

fold to give up one's hand and drop out of the deal.

ante a compulsory stake placed into the pot before the deal

blind bet a compulsory bet made before the deal. It differs from an ante in being an active bet, i.e. it counts towards a better's total stake.

straddle a second and final blind bet made in some poker games. It is larger than the first blind bet.

big blind another name for the straddle.

small blind the first blind bet, which precedes the big blind.

RAISE

Another player puts enough chips into the pot to make his contribution equal to the highest better plus one or more chips. He announces the amount he is putting in, first to call and then to raise. He might say, 'I call two and raise another two.'

FOLD

A player who feels he cannot win returns his cards face down to the dealer and announces that he is folding. This means that the player discards his hand. He relinquishes any interest in the pot for that deal and does not recover any chips he might already have contributed to the pot. Under no circumstances must other players see the cards he held as this would make the game unfair.

When placing chips into the pot, players do not mix their chips with those of the other players, since the value of each player's contribution to the pot must be seen. Players push their chips towards the centre of the table while keeping them separate from the rest.

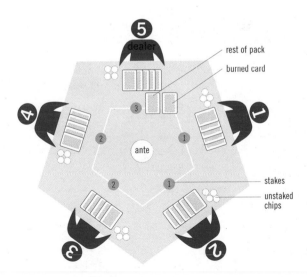

FIRST BETTING ROUND After a first round of betting, a table might look like this; player 1 bets one chip, player 2 calls, player 3 raises, player 4 calls and player 5 re-raises.

EXAMPLE
THE BETTING INTERVAL

A betting interval among seven players, 1, 2, 3, 4, 5, 6 and 7, might proceed as follows.

betting round 1

1 **Player 1 bets one chip.**

2 **Player 2 calls (one chip).**

3 **Player 3 folds.**

4 **Player 4 calls and raises one (two chips).**

5 **Player 5 calls (two chips).**

6 **Player 6 calls (two chips).**

7 **Player 7 calls and raises 2 (four chips).**

betting round 2

The turn to bet now returns to player 1.

1 **Player 1 needs to put in three chips to call, since the highest bet so far is four chips, and 1's contribution to the pot is only one chip. He does this, making his contribution four in total.**

2 **Player 2 folds.**

3 **Player 4 calls by adding two chips to make his contribution four.**

4 **Player 5 raises by putting in four chips, making his contribution six. (He should announce, 'Call two and raise by two.')**

5 **Player 6 folds.**

6 **Player 7 calls by adding two chips to bring his contribution to six.**

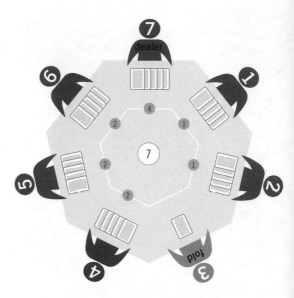

BETTING ROUND 1 The state of play after the first round of betting. Only player 3 has such a poor hand that he folds. The seven chips in the centre is the ante.

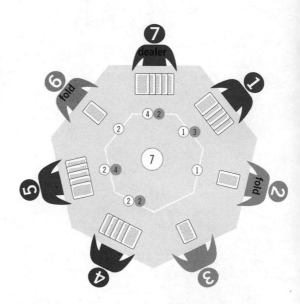

BETTING ROUND 2 After the second betting round, players 2 and 6 also decide to fold as it's not worth risking any more chips on their poor hands.

betting round 3

1 Player 1 also calls by adding two chips to bring his contribution to six.

2 Player 4 folds.

Here the betting interval ends, as all three players who retain an interest in the pot have *equalized* their stakes. The betting interval cannot end until all players in the pot have had an opportunity to bet.

The betting interval described might also be set out as follows, where the figures indicate the number of chips the player put in on each round and (in brackets) the running total of his contribution.

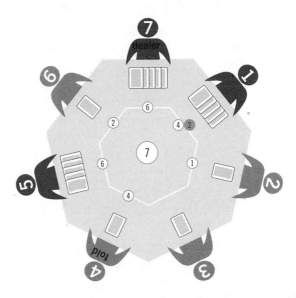

BETTING ROUND 3 The three players remaining have all contributed six chips, so their stakes are equalized.

PLAYERS						
1	2	3	4	5	6	7
FIRST ROUND						
1	1	fold	2	2	2	4
SECOND ROUND						
3(4)	fold		2(4)	4(6)	Fold	2(6)
THIRD ROUND						
2(6)			fold			

Three players – 1, 5 and 7 – retain an interest in the pot, having contributed six chips each, while the pot totals 25 chips.

As mentioned on page 20, in some forms of poker, there is another option in addition to betting, calling, raising or folding – *checking*.

The first player whose turn it is to bet may check, which means he wishes to stay in the pot but not yet to bet, and he doesn't put any chips into the pot. Checking might be thought of as a 'bet of nothing'. Subsequent players may also check, but as soon as any player has made a bet it is no longer possible to check during that betting interval: players can stay in the pot only by calling or raising.

betting after small and big blinds

After blind bets have been made in the form of small and big blinds (say of one and two chips, respectively), the third player (who is the first to bet voluntarily) must put in at least two chips to stay in the pot – i.e. what is needed to call, as the ante and straddle are regarded as normal bets. When the turn to bet has gone round the table and returned to the players who put in the ante and straddle, the chips they contributed count as normal bets: if the stakes are now six chips, player 1 has to contribute only five to call, and player 2 only four.

betting etiquette

To avoid disputes, there are a few general guidelines about betting etiquette. Contravening them can result in penalties (see 'irregularities', page 31).

- A player should always state clearly whether he's betting, folding, raising, calling or checking, e.g. if he is raising, he might say, 'Call two and raise two.'

- Players should always wait for their turn.

- Players should only push their cards away or add them to the discard pile if they are folding.

- In most forms of poker, players should show their cards only during the showdown.

betting limits

It is usually considered desirable to limit the amount that the first better may bet, and the amount by which any player (or players) may raise. This prevents a player with a large bankroll dominating. It is sensible to have a lower limit for a bet or raise and that this limit should be one chip.

It might be, in the most sedate of games, that the upper limit on a bet or raise is also one chip. This is not so stifling or timid as it sounds, as continual raising by four or five players could raise a pot to 50 or more units in the first betting interval, as the table below shows.

		PLAYERS		
1	2	3	4	5
		FIRST ROUND		
1	2	3	4	5
		SECOND ROUND		
5(6)	5(7)	5(8)	5(9)	5(10)
		THIRD ROUND		
5(11)	fold	3(11)	2(11)	fold

On the other hand, if players feel daring or rich, they might decide on the upper limit on a bet or raise equivalent to the value of the highest chip, which might be 10, 25 or 100.

Some also think it desirable to limit the number of raises any one player can make during a betting interval, again as a means of preventing the richest players steamrollering the others. Three raises is a recommended number.

Other ways of establishing upper betting limits are:

variable limit

In Draw Poker the maximum limit might be higher after the draw than before, for example, one chip before the draw, two chips after the draw, or two chips before and five after. In Stud Poker the limit might be higher in the final betting interval than in previous betting intervals for example; in Five-card Stud the limit might be one chip for the first three betting intervals and ten chips for the last.

bet the raise

This means that a player may raise by the greatest number of chips that a previous player has put into the pot. For example, if the first bet was one chip, the limit for a raise is one chip: the first player to raise must put in two chips (one to call and one to raise) – thereafter the limit is two chips, and so on, with the limit rising as the betting progresses. Players do not have to bet up to the limit, but if they were to do so, the stakes would rise rapidly. In the following example, each player either folds, calls or raises by the maximum. In three rounds, the pot reaches 144 chips.

PLAYERS				
1	2	3	4	5
FIRST ROUND				
1	2	2	4	4
SECOND ROUND				
7(8)	14(16)	fold	28(32)	fold
THIRD ROUND				
56(64)	fold		32(64)	

pot limit

With this system, a player may bet or raise by as many chips as are in the pot, which would include the units the player himself needed to put in to call the previous bet. Using this method, the limit can rise very fast. In the following example, each player folds, calls or raises by the maximum.

PLAYERS				
1	2	3	4	5
FIRST ROUND				
1	3	10	34	116
		(total of pot)		
1	4	14	48	164
SECOND ROUND				
394 (395)	fold	385	fold	279
		(total of pot)		
558	558	943	943	1,222

In two rounds, an initial pot of one chip has risen to 1,222 chips.

table stakes

Each player buys an agreed equal amount of chips from the banker, let us say 100 chips. This is called the *take-out*. If a player wants more chips, he must buy them in the same amount of 100 chips, as often as he wishes. He cannot buy additional chips in the middle of a deal, and if he runs out he must wait until after that deal has been won, when he may buy another 100. He can only buy fewer than 100 chips if he cannot afford the full amount. If he then loses these chips he must leave the game. The only limit in this form of poker is the amount of chips a player has before him.

If a player runs out of chips during a deal, he must *tap out* (see page 28).

freeze-out

One form of poker in which the overall amount of stakes that can be lost is limited is called *freeze-out*. In this version all the players begin with an equal number of chips, which has been agreed in advance, and play until only one player is left, who of course wins the lot. No-one can buy more chips during the game. This is a popular form in casinos. Such a game could last an extremely long time.

jargon-buster

tap out a procedure (see page 28) that is forced on a player during a betting interval when he is unable to continue betting because he has insufficient chips to call the bet.

freeze-out a game played to a finish, when only one player is left with all the stake money.

all-in to have all one's chips in the pot.

side-pot a separate pot begun when a player has tapped out.

check to stay in the game without adding to one's total stake. This is not possible once a player has bet at that betting interval.

equalize to make all players' stakes equal. A player who calls equalizes his stake with that of the previous better.

take-out the agreed amount of chips that each player buys from the bank to begin a game at table stakes.

tapping out

One principle of poker is that a player cannot be bulldozed out of a game by heavy betters who increase the stakes beyond his capital. If a player has insufficient chips to call, e.g. if he needs 12 chips to call but has only 10, he may put in all his remaining chips and call for that amount. This is called tapping out. He might say, 'I call for 10 and am tapping out.' Any excess that other players have already contributed is not withdrawn by them, but is moved into a side-pot, kept separate from the main pot, which is thus *equalized*. The player who has tapped out continues in that deal and competes for the main pot, although he takes no further part in the betting itself.

Players still active in the deal continue to bet in the side-pot until their bets are equalized. Should one of them have insufficient chips to call in the side-pot he can tap out of that and a second side-pot is formed. At the showdown, every player who has not folded, including the player who tapped out, competes for the main pot, while the final side-pot is contested only by those players who stayed in and contributed the full amount of chips.

If a player folds in a side-pot, he does not compete for the main pot, even though he folded after the main pot was closed.

The betting interval illustrated has ended with players 3, 4, 5 and 6 as active players in the game, each having contributed 16 chips. Player 2 takes no further part in subsequent betting intervals, but retains his interest in the main pot, which is frozen at 77 chips (players 2, 3, 4, 5 and 6 each having put in 14 chips and the ante being seven chips). Players 3, 4, 5 and 6 withdraw two chips from the main pot each and keep these in a separate pile as the basis for the side-pot. They continue betting at subsequent betting intervals. At the showdown, if player 2's hand is the best remaining, he wins the main pot of 77 chips – if not, he leaves the game. If player 2 takes the 77 chips, the player holding the best hand of those remaining in the side-pot at the showdown takes the side-pot. If his hand is better than player 2's, he takes the main pot and the side-pot.

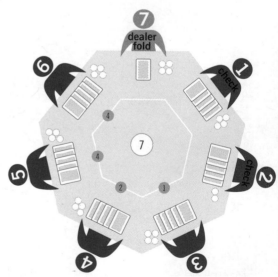

1ST BETTING ROUND Players 1 and 2 aren't sure enough of their hands to bet so check, while the dealer folds.

A player can only tap out if all his chips are exhausted. If he wins the main pot, he can continue in the game, but if he loses he must leave the game, unless table stakes are being played (see page 27), when he can buy another set of chips.

1	2	3	4	5	6	7
			PLAYERS			
			FIRST ROUND			
check	check	1	2	4	4	fold
			SECOND ROUND			
fold	4	7(8)	10(12)	8(12)	12(16)	
			THIRD ROUND			
	10*(14)	8(16)	4(16)	4(16)		

* Player 2 taps out with his remaining 10 chips.

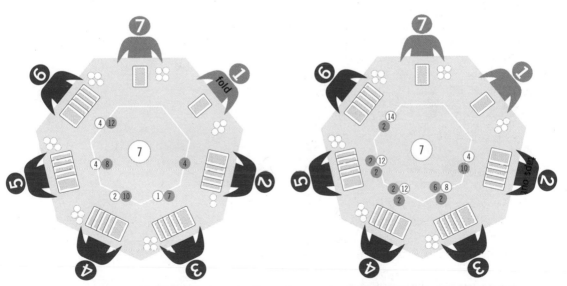

2ND BETTING ROUND Player 1 folds, while player 2 calls player 6's four chips. Player 3 raises the stake to eight chips, player 4 to 12, player 5 calls and player 6 raises to 16 chips.

3RD BETTING ROUND Player 2, with only 10 chips left, taps out with a total of 14 chips, two fewer than he needs to call. Players 3, 4 and 5 add sufficient chips to bring their contributions to the main pot to 14 chips and put two into a side-pot, while 6 takes two chips from his stake and puts those into a side-pot.

showdown

When the final betting interval has taken place, if more than one player is left, they show their hands by exposing them on the table, beginning with the last player to raise. Usually a player announces what he has, e.g. 'Full house, Kings', but it is not necessary to do so, and if he makes a mistake in what he says he is not bound by it – it is the cards that count. The player with the highest-ranking poker hand wins the pot. A player should not begin to take the pot before it is agreed by the others that he has won it.

All players, including those who have folded, are entitled to see the hands of those in the showdown. However, some players, if beaten in the showdown, are reluctant to show their hands in case it provides clues to their strategy, and will say 'You win' or 'Beats me' and fold their cards with the intention of discarding them. Many other players are fine with this, but they can insist on seeing the cards if they wish. To avoid ill-feeling it is best to agree before play starts whether or not all active hands will be exposed at the showdown.

tied hands

If two or more players in the showdown have exactly tied hands (which is very unusual), then the pot is divided between them. If there is an odd chip that cannot be divided, it goes to the player who last raised.

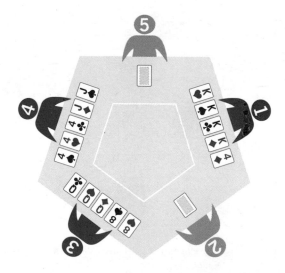

SHOWDOWN Usually all the remaining active hands are shown at the showdown. In this example, players 3 and 4, each with a full house, would have felt confident of winning but are beaten by player 1's 4 Kings.

last man in

If there is only one player remaining in the game (e.g. one player bet or raised and nobody subsequently called) then there is no need for a showdown and that player takes the pot without having to expose his hand.

irregularities

Poker is a game at which large sums of money can change hands, so it is as well to agree a procedure for those irregularities that can happen by accident even among practised card players. The following are recommended actions for certain situations:

misdeals

A deal counts as a misdeal if any of the following happens:

- some cards are found not to be included in the pack.

- some cards in the pack are discovered to be faced, i.e. are face up rather than face down.

- any player points out that the cards weren't properly shuffled and cut.

- the dealer accidentally drops and faces cards.

- more than one player has the wrong number of cards.

The deal is cancelled and the dealer loses his turn. The deal passes to the next player. The cards must be shuffled and cut again before the new deal. Any antes in the pot remain, and are duplicated by the antes properly made for the next pot. By prior agreement, misdeals cancelled because of the dealer's error may incur a fine on him, say one chip to each player.

Other errors are less serious and do not result in a misdeal.

- If a dealer makes a mistake during the deal which can be easily rectified, such as accidentally dealing a card to the wrong player, he can correct it by transferring the card as necessary.

- If a dealer omits a player in the deal he must give his own hand to the omitted player. If he deals a hand too many, the excess hand becomes dead, i.e. it is discarded and put to one side.

- Players should count their cards before looking at them, and if a player finds he has a card too few, the dealer should give him the top card of the pack. If a player has a card too many, the last card dealt is returned to dealer and is dead.

betting errors

BETTING OUT OF TURN

Betting out of turn is an annoying error in poker games. If a player makes a bet, raises or calls out of turn, his call is 'frozen' for the moment, as are any chips he put into the pot, i.e. the call is remembered until the player's turn comes round, when it is dealt with as detailed below. Whatever happens, he may not remove the chips from the pot. The player whose turn it properly was, and any succeeding player, takes his turn as if the out-of-turn player had not spoken. When it becomes the turn of the offending player, he is limited in his actions.

- If he bet, and there has been no previous bet in that betting interval, then he is deemed to have made the bet as specified.

- If there has been an intervening bet, then he is deemed to have called. If the chips he put in are insufficient for the call, he must either add to them to make them so, or fold and forfeit them to the pot. If the chips were more than required for the call, then he is still deemed to have called, but the surplus chips remain in the pot and are forfeited. He may not raise.

- If a player folds out of turn, and there are two or more players before him who have yet to act, then that player must put in enough chips to call any raise made by those preceding players, although he is then deemed to have folded and so cannot win the pot. If the intervening players call or fold, the offending player's fold is allowed and he does not face a penalty.

NOT ENOUGH CHIPS

If a player makes a bet or call, whether it is his turn or not, and does not put any chips into the pot, then his announcement is void.

If he puts in insufficient chips for his bet or call, then he must on demand put in the extra chips to satisfy his announcement.

TOO MANY CHIPS

If he puts in too many chips then his announcement stands and the extra chips are forfeited to the pot, unless he corrects his announcement before another player points out the error.

When a wrong announcement is made or a player bets out of turn, once chips have been contributed to the pot they cannot be removed.

exposing cards

A player who folds must not expose his cards – in fact cards should not be exposed unless the rules require it in the showdown. A player who accidentally exposes a card is not penalized, but a player who exposes cards regularly, whether intentionally or not, should pay a penalty on request of the dealer – say one chip to each player.

going through the discards

No player may look at the cards remaining in the pack after the deal is completed, nor at cards discarded by players during the deal. A player who does so, if still in the game, must fold; if not in the game he must pay a penalty – say one chip to each player.

dealer's responsibility

The dealer should watch for irregularities and draw the attention of the players to any that might occur. Any dispute in the action to be taken should be decided by the players.

using wild cards

Wild cards can be used in all forms of poker. Originally the Joker was added to the pack and used as a wild card, i.e. the holder of the Joker (usually called 'the bug') could use it to represent any card he wished.

Nowadays it is more common to specify all cards of a particular rank as wild. In the Draw Poker variation Spit in the Ocean (see page 72), all cards of the rank of the spit are wild.

Most commonly it is the 2s that are specified as wild – 'deuces wild'. If only two wild cards are wanted, either black 2s or the 'one-eyed' Jacks (♥J and ♠J) are used. If three wild cards are wanted, then all 'one-eyed' picture cards are used, adding the ♦K to the ♥J and ♠J.

PROBABILITIES

Using wild cards upsets all the probabilities of holding specific hands, shown in the next chapter. It also alters the values of particular hands and in some cases reverses them. For instance, with deuces wild three of a kind becomes a more probable hand to be dealt than two pairs, and four of a kind more likely than a flush. If a hand contains one wild card, it is impossible for the hand to be two pairs but no better, because for the hand to be two pairs it must include one natural pair, and if it includes one natural pair the wild card makes the pair into three of a kind, i.e. if you had ♥9, ♦9, ♠8, ♠2 and ♦3, it would be better to add the deuce to the pair of 9s and make three of a kind rather than two pairs.

But despite two pairs without a wild card being more difficult to achieve than three of a kind, the ranking of the hands does not change.

As a guide to how playing poker with deuces wild affects the probability of being dealt certain

hands, Table 2 opposite shows how dramatically some of them have changed.

When assessing hands in games where deuces are wild, it is worth knowing that with five or six players, the average winning hand is three Aces, one of which will be a wild card. It is also worth bearing in mind that holding a 'natural' combination will not be so good as holding the same combination with a deuce or two, because your holding a deuce reduces the number of wild cards available for other players and increases the odds against them holding one. In fact with four wild cards in the pack it is seldom worth contesting a pot oneself without holding a wild card. The probability is that the pot will be won by at least three of a kind, so it is not wise to call with anything less.

WHAT BEATS WHAT?

It is essential when using wild cards to agree on 'tied' combinations of the same rank. There are two schools of thought:

1 This school values any hand at face value as if it did not include a wild card – thus for example 9–8–W–6–5 is a straight, nine high, and beats 7–6–5–4–3, which is straight, seven high.

2 This school values a hand without a wild card higher than a hand which contains a wild card, and would thus say that where straights are concerned 7–6–5–4–3 beats 9–8–W–6–5. It would also say that a hand with one wild card beats a similarly ranked hand with two wild

cards, thus A–A–W–6–3 beats A–W–W–10–4, whereas the first school would say the latter was better. In fact those who rate hands with the fewest wild cards as high within each rank of hand would say 7–7–7–Q–8 would beat both hands containing three Aces, since the hands with the Aces required more wild cards.

These are questions that have to be agreed before play – it is likely to cause problems if the only decision is 'deuces wild', because that will soon lead to the question of how to compare hands like those listed above.

WHAT CAN WILD CARDS REPRESENT?

If wild cards are used, another question must be decided: can they be used only as cards which the holder does not already hold, or can they be used to duplicate a card. At the beginning of this book it was stated that in some schools a wild card could represent any card a player wishes, except one that he already holds, and this seems the most sensible use of wild cards. However, some players prefer a wild card to represent any card, even one already in the hand.

FIVE OF A KIND

This preference introduces a new hand, i.e. five of a kind. A player who holds four 8s and a wild card, or three 8s and two wild cards can announce a hand of five 8s. As there are only four suits, two of the 8s must be of the same suit. So where does five of a kind rank among the classes of hand? Some schools rank five of a kind as the highest hand, and others rank it as second to a royal flush (A, K, Q, J, 10 of a suit). This classes a royal flush as a separate class of hand to a straight flush, whereas of course it is in fact the highest straight flush. So that is illogical.

When one wild card is used – the Joker or bug – it is even more illogical to rate the royal flush as

Hand	Probability without wild cards	Probability with deuces wild
One pair	1 in 2.4	1 in 2.1
Two pairs	1 in 21	1 in 27
Three of a kind	1 in 47	1 in 7
Straight	1 in 255	1 in 39
Flush	1 in 509	1 in 197
Full house	1 in 694	1 in 205
Four of a kind	1 in 4,165	1 in 84
Straight flush	1 in 69,974	1 in 638
Five of a kind	n/a	1 in 3868
Royal flush	1 in 649,740	1 in 5370

TABLE 2: Probability of holding certain hands

higher than five of a kind since it is the commoner hand by a ratio of 24 to 13.

DOUBLE-ACE FLUSH

There is another 'false' hand to consider when wild cards are used, i.e. the double-Ace flush. If a player holds ♥A, ♥9, ♥8, ♥3, W, then the wild card could be classed as the ♥A and a double-Ace flush appears. This would beat a flush consisting of ♦A, ♦K, ♦Q, ♦J, ♦9. If you had two wild cards, a treble-Ace flush would be possible, of course. There are some players who will recognize five of a kind but not a double-Ace flush, which is illogical. Couple the question of whether double-Ace flushes are allowable with the question of whether between two flushes a hand with fewer wild cards beats a hand with more, and one can see that the use of wild cards is not straightforward.

draw poker

In early poker games, players were dealt five cards upon which they bet. There was no provision for a player to change any of his cards – it was a game of deal, bet, showdown. When the concept was introduced of allowing players, after what now became the first betting interval, to improve their hands by discarding some cards and drawing others to replace them, before a second round of betting took place, the game became called 'Draw Poker' to distinguish it from the earlier game, which is now not widely played at all. Nowadays the name 'Draw Poker' is retained to distinguish it from forms of Stud Poker. It remains the most common form of poker played at home and beginners are advised to master it before attempting Stud, Hold 'Em, etc.

The version described first is the basic game, which might be called 'Straight Draw Poker' but in the USA a slight variation called 'Jackpots' (see page 68) is so popular that some American books will describe that as the main game, and this version as a variation, called something like 'Anything Opens'. 'Draw' is a slight misnomer, since players do not 'draw' their replacement cards, which are dealt to them by the dealer. The game is best for between five and seven players.

preliminaries

As described before in the general rules for poker games, players should agree a few things before they start playing:

- a time limit for the game, and agree that when that time is reached the game ends as soon as all the players have dealt an equal number of times.

- which form of the game is being played (as will be seen, there are hundreds of variations, one of which is called Dealer's Choice, which allows the dealer to choose which variation will be played for that deal).

- the stake limits.

- how any irregularities are to be dealt with.

- who is to be banker if chips are being used.

- who is to be first dealer.

- seating arrangements.

For this description of a six-handed game, we will assume the following have been agreed:

- chips of four colours, valued at one, two, five and 10 units, are being used.

- no bet or raise may be less than one chip.

- before the draw no raise may be larger than two chips, and after the draw five chips.

- the maximum number of raises one player can make is three per betting interval.

the play

1 The dealer places six chips in the centre of the table as an ante to start the pot. This represents one chip for each player, but for convenience each dealer in turn may ante for all players.

2 The cards are shuffled and dealt as described in the general rules of the game above.

3 The dealer gives five cards to each player, one at a time, and including himself, beginning with the player to his left (sometimes called the eldest hand). The dealer then places the remainder of the pack face down in front of him.

first betting interval

Between deals, players have the opportunity to bet in 'betting intervals', which may be divided into 'betting rounds'. The first opportunity to bet lies with the player to dealer's left. He has three choices at this stage: to fold, to check or to bet. If he checks, the second player has the same option, and so on. But as soon as one player has bet, the option to check ends – from then on players must either call, raise or fold.

If every player, including the dealer, checks on the first round, the deal comes to an end. The cards are collected, reshuffled and cut, and dealt by the next dealer, who puts in another ante of six chips, making the pot twelve chips for the next deal.

the draw

The betting interval ends when the bets of all the players who remain in the game are equalized. The draw then takes place.

1 The dealer takes up the undealt portion of the pack, and deals in turn with each player who remains in the game, i.e. those who haven't folded, beginning with the player nearest to his left.

2 This player announces how many cards he wishes to discard. If he does not wish to change his hand, he is said to 'stand pat'. This is usually done by announcing 'none' and tapping on the table. Otherwise he may discard between one and three cards. (If there were fewer than six players, he could discard up to four cards.)

3 The player passes the discards face down to the dealer who lays them to one side to make a discard pile. He then gives the player an equal number of cards to restore his hand to five cards.

4 The dealer then deals similarly with the next player. No player need announce how many he wishes to discard until the previous player has been dealt with.

5 The dealer draws his own cards last, taking care to announce how many cards he is discarding and replacing.

During the draw, before the first bet has been made, any player may enquire of another how many cards he drew.

second betting interval

When the draw is completed, and all players have their final hands of five cards each, the second betting interval takes place. The first player to speak is the first player who bet on the first betting interval. If he has subsequently folded, then the first active player to his left has the same opportunity, and so on. The first options are to check, fold or bet, as before, but once a bet has been made, then subsequently the options are to fold, call or raise. Again the betting round continues until all active players have contributed the same amount to the pot, when the betting stops and the showdown takes place.

the showdown

Starting with the last player to raise, and continuing clockwise, each active player shows and announces his hand. The player who holds the best poker hand takes the pot.

EXAMPLE
A BASIC HAND

There are six players. Player 1 puts in an ante of six chips and deals five cards to each player.

first betting interval

FIRST BETTING ROUND

1 **Player 2, with a pair of 7s, checks.**

2 **Player 3, with a chance of a straight, checks.**

3 **Player 4, with a pair of Kings, bets one chip.**

4 **Player 5, with two pairs, 6s and 5s, calls and raises two (i.e. he puts in three chips).**

5 **Player 6, without a pair, folds.**

6 **Player 1, with a pair of Jacks, calls.**

SECOND BETTING ROUND

1 **Player 2, with two players having staked three chips, doesn't fancy his small pair and folds.**

2 **Player 3, however, calls with three chips.**

3 **Player 4, who already has one chip in the pot, calls by putting in another two chips.**

Players 3, 4, 5 and 1 have now equalized their stakes by putting in three chips, so the first betting interval ends. The pot holds 18 chips.

the draw

1 **Player 3 discards his ♦4, hoping to draw a Queen or 7, and draws ♦7, giving him a straight.**

2 **Player 4 keeps his two Kings and discards his other cards. He draws ♠10, ♥10, ♦8, so now holds two pairs, Kings and 10s.**

3 **Player 5 draws one, discarding ♥3, and hoping for a 6 or a 5, but unluckily he gets ♠7. Player 1 announces that he is drawing two cards. He discards ♥4 and ♠2, and receives ♦Q and ♠5, so does not significantly improve his hand.**

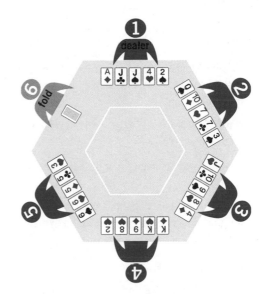

1ST BETTING ROUND   Players 2 and 3 check and player 6's bad hand gives him no choice but to fold.

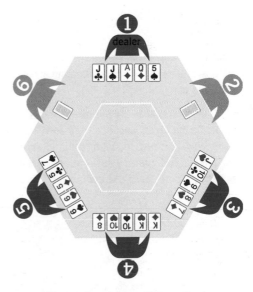

THE DRAW   Players 3 and 4 benefit from the draw, while players 5 and 1 do not.

second betting interval

FIRST BETTING ROUND

1 The first player to bet in the first betting interval, player 4, is the first to speak. He bets one chip on his two pairs, making his total stake four chips.

2 Player 5, with his two pairs, calls by adding a chip to his stake.

3 Player 1, with a solitary pair of Jacks, decides to fold.

4 Player 3, who has a straight, calls for one chip and raises by two, bringing his stake in the pot to six chips.

SECOND BETTING ROUND

1 Player 4, who thinks it is quite likely that player 3, like himself, has two pairs, thinks it is worth staying in with his Kings and 10s, and calls, putting in two chips.

2 Player 5, who also has two pairs, but with the higher pair only 6s, thinks he is beaten and folds.

showdown

The stakes are now equal so the showdown takes place, player 3, with his straight beating player 4, with his two pairs.

Player 3 therefore takes the pot, which totals 25 chips. As he put in six, plus one (in theory) for the ante, he wins 18 chips. Including their antes, player 2 loses one, player 4 loses seven, player 5 loses five, player 6 loses one and player 1, the dealer, loses four.

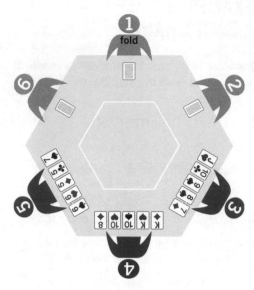

1ST BETTING ROUND Player 1 did not improve his hand in the draw, so his best option is to fold.

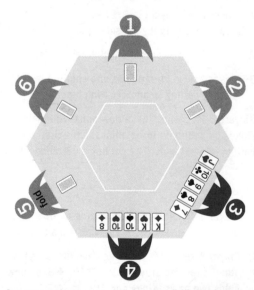

2ND BETTING ROUND AND SHOWDOWN Player 5 didn't improve his hand in the draw, so his best option is to fold. Player 3's straight beats player 4's two pairs.

the arithmetic of draw poker

In Table 1 (see pages 12–13), the number of ranking poker hands, and how often they are likely to be dealt, were shown. From these you can estimate the value of any hand as dealt. For example, almost exactly half of all hands will include at least one pair. However, a player will not receive a hand better than this more than roughly 7.5 per cent of the time, or about once in 13 hands. Table 3 gives the chances of being dealt each hand or better.

TABLE 3: Probability of holding any particular hand or better in five cards dealt

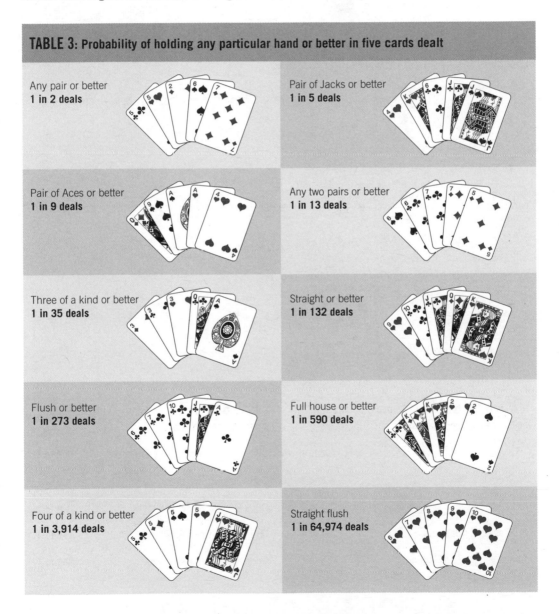

Any pair or better
1 in 2 deals

Pair of Jacks or better
1 in 5 deals

Pair of Aces or better
1 in 9 deals

Any two pairs or better
1 in 13 deals

Three of a kind or better
1 in 35 deals

Straight or better
1 in 132 deals

Flush or better
1 in 273 deals

Full house or better
1 in 590 deals

Four of a kind or better
1 in 3,914 deals

Straight flush
1 in 64,974 deals

TABLE 4: Probability in percentages of holding the best hand at the deal

		Number of players						
		2	3	4	5	6	7	8
Pair of Jacks		79%	63%	50%	40%	32%	25%	20%
Pair of Aces		89%	79%	70%	62%	55%	49%	43%
Two pairs		93%	86%	80%	74%	68%	63%	59%
Three of a kind		98%	94%	92%	89%	87%	84%	82%

TABLE 5: Probability of improving one pair by drawing three cards

Odds against any improvement	2.4 to 1
Odds against two pairs	4.8 to 1
Odds against three of a kind	7.7 to 1
Odds against full house	97 to 1
Odds against four of a kind	359 to 1

TABLE 6: Probability of improving one pair by drawing two cards

Odds against any improvement	2.8 to 1
Odds against two pairs	4.8 to 1
Odds against three of a kind	11.9 to 1
Odds against full house	119 to 1
Odds against four of a kind	1080 to 1

If being dealt two pairs is to receive a good hand, in that you will equal or beat it only once in 13 times, how likely is it that you will be holding the best hand if you are one of six players? The answer is approximately 68 per cent of the time, or odds of slightly better than 2 to 1 on that you hold the best hand.

Table 4 gives an indication of how good the hand you are dealt with is, up to three of a kind, in terms of how likely it is to be the best hand dealt.

From this table it can be seen that if you are dealt three of a kind, the chance of you holding the best hand at that stage is 82 per cent (better than 4 to 1 on) even if there are eight players in the game.

odds of improving a hand in the draw

The better the hand you are dealt, the lower the odds of you improving it in the draw; the chances of improving your three of a kind in the draw are more than 8 to 1 against.

Usually the number of cards to exchange at the draw is obvious and straightforward. However, many poker players have differing views on the advisability of drawing two or three cards when holding a pair. Some players, with a hand like ♠A, ♥10, ♣3, ♦3, ♥2 would prefer to hold the pair and the ♠A (the odd card in this situation is called a kicker (see below) rather than draw three cards to the pair. Tables 5 and 6 indicate the approximate probability of improving the hand drawing either two or three cards. From these it can be seen that by drawing three cards to a pair, the chance of improving the hand is about 14 per cent better than if only two cards are drawn. However, more than half the time, the improvement will be to two pairs only (57 per cent with a draw of three and 66 per cent with a draw of two).

kickers

This shows why some players advise keeping the high card as a kicker rather than discarding it. If the player who held the ♠A, ♥10, ♣3, ♦3, ♥2, ended with two pairs, then it is to be hoped that he kept his Ace kicker and drew two cards only, because if he had it is odds on that his top pair will be Aces, and if two pairs is to win the deal, to have two Aces almost guarantees success.

On balance, of course, the tables show that it is better to draw three cards to a pair rather than two (provided there are no other possibilities to consider, such as a flush), but a good player will choose to hold a pair and a kicker from time to time in order to keep his opponents in doubt as to his habits. It is probably not worth keeping a kicker unless it is an Ace or King.

improving three of a kind

Some players occasionally consider keeping a kicker when holding three of a kind. The chances of improving the hand are better if two cards are drawn, but the odds are interesting, as Tables 7 and 8 show.

The interesting thing here is that by drawing two cards you more or less halve the odds against you of improving to four of a kind, but at the expense of slightly extending the odds against you of making a full house.

In this case, however, psychology comes in. A player who draws one card is often attempting to fill to a flush or straight, or to improve two pairs to full house. If a player bets heavily after drawing one card other players might assume he has succeeded in achieving one of those hands, since if he fails his hand will be no better than two pairs. Therefore a player who draws one card to three of a kind and fails, by betting heavily might persuade other players that he has at least a straight and win the pot by bluff.

improving to flush, straight or full house

The approximate odds of improving to flush, straight or full house by drawing one card is shown in Table 9.

It can be seen that an opponent drawing one card and hoping to fill a straight flush, flush, straight or full house never has a better chance than just over 2 to 1 against. Indeed, unless he holds four cards which could make a straight flush (once in about 500 hands) then his chances of improvement are never better than over 4 to 1 against (not counting an improvement to one pair).

Table 9 also reveals that holding four cards to a flush, you have only a little worse than a 4 to 1 against chance of completing a flush with the draw. No skilled poker player would think of drawing two cards when holding three of the same suit, hoping to fill in a flush. The odds are about 23 to 1. The odds are about the same of filling to a straight when holding three cards in sequence – it is simply not worth attempting.

TABLE 7: Probability of improving three of a kind drawing two cards	
Odds against any improvement	8.6 to 1
Odds against full house	15.4 to 1
Odds against four of a kind	22.5 to 1

TABLE 8: Probability of improving three of a kind drawing one card	
Odds against any improvement	10.8 to 1
Odds against full house	14.7 to 1
Odds against four of a kind	46 to 1

TABLE 9: Probability of improving certain hands by drawing one card

Four-card hand held		Improved final hand	Odds against
Double-ended straight flush (i.e. you could add a card to either end)		Straight flush Flush Straight Any of above	**22.6 to 1** **5.8 to 1** **6.8 to 1** **2.1 to 1**
Straight flush with single end or gap in middle (i.e. there is only one value card you can add)		Straight flush Flush Straight Any of above	**46 to 1** **4.9 to 1** **14.7 to 1** **2.9 to 1**
Four-card flush		Flush	**4.2 to 1**
Double-ended straight (i.e. you could add a card to either end)		Straight	**4.9 to 1**
Straight with single end or gap in middle (i.e. there is only one value card you can add)		Straight	**10.8 to 1**
Two pairs		Full house	**10.8 to 1**

the odds opposed to the pot

Players should have an idea of the odds against improving a hand at the draw so that they don't bet more than their 'expectation'. The expectation is the amount a gambler stands to win multiplied by his probability of winning it.

PROBABILITIES

Probabilities are expressed by a number between 0 (impossibility) to 1 (certainty), thus when tossing a true coin the probability of it falling a head or a tail is 0.5 heads and 0.5 tails. So if a gambler were asked to stake 10 chips on his choice, and to receive 20 if correct, the game would be fair. The pay-out is 20, the probability is 0.5, so the expectation is 20 x 0.5, which equals 10. As 10 is the stake, the game is a perfectly fair one.

For a slightly more complex example imagine a pack of cards stripped of the picture cards, so that the pack contains Aces to 10s only. The gambler is asked to cut the shuffled pack, and whatever card is turned up he will be paid that number of chips, i.e. one chip for an Ace up to ten chips for a 10. What should he pay for each turn? The question is worked out as follows.

Suppose he took 40 tries and cut each card once, which is what the law of large numbers suggests will happen over the long run, he will receive:

- one chip four times (for Aces).

- two chips four times (for 2s).

- and so on up to ten chips four times (for 10s).

The total return is 220 chips. If he receives 220 chips over 40 trials, for it to be a fair game he should pay 220 divided by 40 – 5.5 chips per try. If he pays five chips per try, over the long run he wins; if he pays six, he loses.

---

always work out your expectation

Do not bet unless the odds being paid to you are greater than the odds against making the hand. Suppose you hold two pairs, and think you will win if you can improve to a full house. Table 9 shows the odds against this are 10.8 to 1, i.e. there are almost 11 chances of failure to one of success. Your chance of success is one in 12. If the pot is 60 chips, your expectation is 60 x $\frac{1}{12}$: 5. If it costs you five chips or fewer to call, it is worth betting, if it costs you six chips or more, it is less worth it. Looked at another way, if the odds against winning the pot are 11 to 1, and it costs you five chips to call, the pot should be worth at least 55 chips for you to bet.

EXAMPLE QUESTIONS TO ASK YOURSELF

You are dealer. There are six players and therefore six chips in the pot as ante. You hold ♥J, ♠9, ♦8, ♣7, ♥6.

The first player checks, the second bets one chip, the third calls one and raises another, the fourth calls the two and raises two more, the fifth folds.

There are 13 chips in the pot, and to stay in it will cost you four chips to call. You have a chance of a straight. You would need to discard the Jack, and draw either a 10 or a 5. You need to bear the following in mind:

WHAT IS THE POT?

Should you be successful, you stand to win a pot which at the moment stands at 13 chips.

WHAT ARE THE ODDS AGAINST GETTING YOUR CARD?

From the Table 9 (page 47), you can see the odds are approximately 5 to 1 against you drawing a 10 or a 5 (one chance in six, or one-sixth).

WHAT DOES THIS MAKE YOUR EXPECTANCY?

So your expectancy is roughly one-sixth of 13, or just over two chips.

WHAT WOULD YOU NEED TO STAKE?

Your stake has to be four chips. This is a bad bet, and you should fold.

Let us examine this further. There are still two things you do not know.

1 How many players will stay in after the first betting interval. If all the other players still in equalized their stakes, so that four others as well as you raised their stakes to four chips, there would be a pot of 26 chips, making your expectancy a fraction better than your stake of

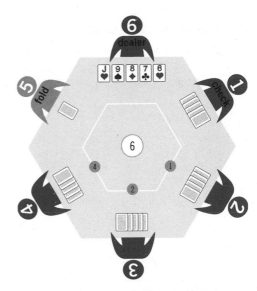

WHAT IS YOUR EXPECTANCY? When deciding how to bet, you need to weigh the odds of winning against how many chips you must put in and the size of the pot.

four chips. But of course all except the last to raise might fold.

2 Whether you would win if you did fill your straight. Two other players have already raised, and could have good hands themselves. If you do not fill your straight, your best possible hand would be a pair of 9s, and it is pretty certain you will not win with that.

GOING STRAIGHT

If it would be wise in the circumstances above to fold rather than call, how much wiser would it be if you were thinking of drawing to an 'inside straight' – one with a gap in the middle, such as ♥10, ♠9, ♦8, ♥6, ♣2. The odds against you filling are twice as long. How is there ever going to be a pot where there are about 12 times the number of chips in the pot as you need to bet?

how many cards to draw?

Table 10 recommends how many cards to draw with each holding from one pair to a four-card, double-ended straight flush and the chances of improving in terms of probability and approximate odds.

TABLE 10: Recommended draws and chances of improvement

Cards held	Number of cards to draw	Improvement to	Probability (1 = 100%)	Approx odds against
One pair	3	Two pairs	0.171	4.8 to 1
		Three of a kind	0.114	7.7 to 1
		Full house	0.010	97 to 1
		Four of a kind	0.003	359 to 1
		Any improvement	0.298	2.4 to 1
One pair with Ace	2	Two pairs (Aces up)	0.117	7.6 to 1
		Two pairs (not Aces)	0.056	17 to 1
		Three of a Kind	0.078	11.9 to1
		Full house (Aces up)	0.003	359 to 1
		Full house (not Aces up)	0.006	179 to 1
		Four of a kind	0.001	1080 to 1
		Any improvement	0.261	2.8 to 1
Two pairs	1	Full house	0.085	10.8 to 1
Three of a kind	2	Full house	0.061	15.4 to 1
		Four of a kind	0.043	22.5 to 1
		Any improvement	0.104	8.6 to 1

Cards held		Number of cards to draw	Improvement to	Probability	Approx. odds against
Double-ended straight		1	Straight	0.170	4.9 to 1
Straight with single end or gap in middle		1	Straight	0.085	10.8 to 1
Four-card flush		1	Flush	0.191	4.2 to 1
Double-ended straight flush		1	Straight flush	0.043	22.5 to 1
			Flush	0.148	5.8 to 1
			Straight	0.128	6.8 to 1
			Any improvement	0.318	2.1 to 1
Straight flush with single end or gap in middle		1	Straight flush	0.021	46 to 1
			Flush	0.170	4.9 to 1
			Straight	0.064	14.7 to 1
			Any improvement	0.255	2.9 to 1

TABLE 11: Value of each hand at the first betting interval

Hand held	Number of variations	Number of better hands	Number of better hands (per cent)
Straight flush	40	0	0
Fours	624	40	0.002
Full house	3,744	664	0.025
Flush	5,108	4,408	0.170
Straight	10,200	9,516	0.336
Three of a kind	54,912	19,716	0.759
Two pairs	123,552	74,628	2.872
Pair of Aces	84,480	198,180	7.625
Pair of Kings	84,480	282,660	10.876
Pair of Queens	84,480	376,140	14.473
Pair of Jacks	84,480	451,620	17.377
Pair of 10s	84,480	536,100	20.627
Pair of 9s to pair of 2s	675,840	620,580	23.878
No pair	1,302,540	1,296,420	49.882

values of hands containing a single pair

We have not considered so far the comparative value of hands that hold a single pair and, since a hand containing a pair will beat half the hands dealt before the first betting interval, and a pair of 10s will beat roughly four out of every five, it is worth considering the status of a single pair. Table 11 shows the values of hands down to no pair, by giving the percentage of hands that will be better at the deal. For example, a pair of Jacks will be beaten at the deal by just 17 per cent of opposing hands, or fewer than one in five, while a pair of Aces will be beaten by less than eight per cent, or fewer than one in twelve.

strategy before the draw

The first decision you have to make after the deal is whether to fold, check, call, bet or raise. In making this decision you will naturally be assessing your hand, at the same time deciding which cards you will discard in the draw if you remain in the deal that long. The cards to discard will almost always be obvious but it is essential that you do not set them aside or rearrange your hand by putting them to one end of the fan or in any other way give other players a clue as to how many you intend to discard. There's no point in giving away any information before you have to.

where are you sitting?

In some positions at the table you might not get the opportunity to check, and in fact wherever you sit your position relative to the dealer will affect how you act. Suppose, for example, you are dealt a hand like ♠J, ♥J, ♦8, ♣5, ♥4 – a pair of Jacks. Look back at Table 4 (page 44). It shows that if you are one of six players, you have a 32 per cent chance of holding the best hand at the table.

EXAMPLE
ON THE DEALER'S LEFT

If you are on the dealer's left, and hold this hand you would not wish to fold. You have two options:

(A) BET

There are six chips already in the pot (the ante) and with the hand dealt your current chances of winning it are little worse than 2 to 1 against, so you could bet. If you bet, it is possible that all players with a hand smaller than yours at the deal will fold, because many players don't risk adding chips to the pot if somebody has already bet and their own hands are worth less than a pair of Jacks. This would mean that in about a third of the cases, you could win the pot immediately.

(B) CHECK

This keeps your options open. Suppose by the time the betting reaches you again, one other player has checked, one has bet, and three have folded. With seven chips in the pot, it might be worth a chip to call. This might get rid of the other player who called, leaving you with one opponent for a pot that starts at eight chips.

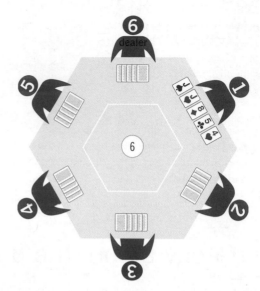

TO THE DEALER'S LEFT With a pair of Jacks, player 1 has a one-in-three chance of currently holding the best hand, so it is worth risking a bet with six chips in the pot.

EXAMPLE
ON THE DEALER'S RIGHT (A)

Suppose you are dealt the same hand but are now the player to the dealer's right. One player has bet one chip, another has raised to two and a third has called, making a total of 11 chips in the pot. Do you call, raise or fold?

You need to put in two chips to call. You reason that there are three players (the dealer has yet to speak) who probably have better hands than a pair of Jacks. If you assume that a pair of Jacks or better is needed to start betting in a game of six or more players, then the player who opened the

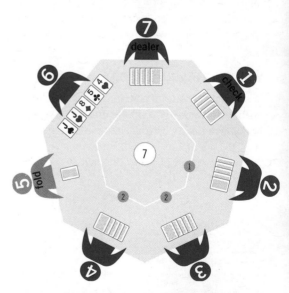

TO THE DEALER'S RIGHT (A) The other players' bets indicate to player 6 that they probably have better hands and to fold would be wisest.

betting has a reasonably high pair at least, that the player who raised is unlikely to hold less than a pair of Aces, as is the player who called. Your pair of Jacks does not look so good now. It is quite likely that one of your opponents has three of a kind. Table 5 (page 44) tells you that the odds against you improving your hand to three of a kind at the draw are approximately eight to one.

Betting two chips to win 11 is not an attractive proposition and you would be advised now to fold and wait for a better chance.

With this hand in these circumstances you should not raise.

EXAMPLE
TO THE DEALER'S RIGHT (B)

On the other hand, if you are sitting at dealer's right and all the players before you have checked or folded, your pair of Jacks is certainly worth betting, with only the dealer to come. Table 11 (page 52) shows that as only just over 20 per cent of hands are better than a pair of Jacks, your chances of having a better hand than the dealer are 4 to 1 on, so bet. Since almost half of all hands dealt do not include a pair at all, it is worth betting in this position with any pair. The players who checked now have to enter the betting or fold.

what cards could you stay in with?

QUEENS

If we assume that a pair of Jacks is worth staying in the game with if nobody before you has opened, what hand would you need to stay in with if you are facing a previous bet (i.e. there has been a bet but not a raise)? If the stakes are limited, you would usually stay in with a pair of Queens or better, and raise with a pair of Aces or better.

ACES

A pair of Aces is a good hand to hold at the deal, as Table 4 (page 44) shows (if there are five players, there is a 62 per cent chance that your hand is at the moment the best). If a pair eventually wins the pot, then your Aces (unless another player also has a pair of Aces) will win. Similarly if you improve to two pairs, and two pairs wins the pot, you will almost certainly win. If you improve to a third Ace, it will take a straight or better to beat you. Aces are good news. You could also raise with a pair of Kings, according to whether or not you are a 'loose' or 'tight' player, and how you view your opponents.

If before you bet a previous player has bet and another has raised, then you need at least a pair of Aces to stay in.

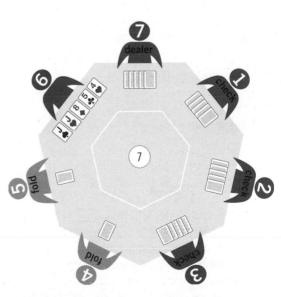

TO THE DEALER'S RIGHT (B)   As the previous five players have declined to bet, player 6 knows that it is worth betting on his two Jacks.

tight player

A 'tight' player is a player who will only bet when he has a good hand, and is prepared to wait for one to come along.

loose player

A 'loose' player is one who will sometimes get impatient to be in the action and bet somewhat impetuously. A good player will be aware of the temperaments of his opponents, and will act accordingly, at the same time, of course, trying to play a varied game himself.

If a player is known to be a tight player, whenever he suddenly starts to bet on a hand, an aware opponent will know he holds something worthwhile and will rapidly fold where maybe he might have risked a chip or two on a moderate hand. When among good players the tight player will, therefore, win fewer chips when he gets a good hand than he might have done had he previously shown more inclination to take a chance.

Similarly a loose player, known to bet on straights or flushes of three cards, hoping to draw two cards to fill, will not scare anybody into folding.

In most poker games, which are played among friends and are primarily social gatherings rather than attempts to make some quick riches, players will tend to be on the loose side. This makes for better entertainment, and pots might be larger than they would be in a stricter environment. A tight player carefully calculating the odds in these situations risks being regarded as a trifle unsporting.

what do your opponents' bets tell you?

Unless there is some bluffing going on, the first player to bet has possibly a pair of Jacks or better and the raiser quite likely a pair of Aces or better.

call or raise?

So you might reason that to call and contribute at least two chips to the pot you need at least a couple of pairs.

It would be rash to raise yourself without holding three of a kind (of any rank). If before you get a chance to bet there has already been a bet and two raises then perhaps a middling three of a kind would be required to stay in, and a high one, such as Aces, to raise.

If you have already bet yourself, and you face a raise, then call with a pair of Aces or better, but do not re-raise without at least two pairs, with Jacks as the higher. If you have bet and two players have subsequently raised, then do not stay in without three of a kind.

pot limit

If you are playing pot limit (see page 26), then the stakes required can rise rapidly if players raise and re-raise, and you might require better hands than those mentioned in the text to stay in or raise.

how to lose money quickly

In preceding tables, particularly Table 10, we have listed chances of improving hands at the draw, and we make no excuses for repeating the idea that betting heavily on a hand that could be a good one after the draw, but is worthless as it stands, is one of the commonest ways for inexperienced players to lose plenty of cash.

It is, as an example, never worth betting with a hand like J, 8, 7, 6, 4 of assorted suits, where the only chance of improving, albeit to a very good hand, is to discard the Jack and hope to draw a 5 for a straight. The odds against success are nearly 11 to 1, and the pot will never justify such a gamble. From this example, the general principle can be drawn that relying optimistically on a draw is a dangerous tactic.

EXAMPLE
RISKY BUSINESS

This deal involves six players, therefore there are six chips in the pot. The limit is one chip to bet or raise before the draw, two chips after the draw. Player 1 is the dealer and you are player 6.

first betting interval

FIRST BETTING ROUND

1 **Player 2 checks, as do 3 and 4.**

2 **Player 5 opens with his pair of Queens, making the pot up to seven chips.**

3 **As player 6, you can guess that players 2, 3 and 4 probably hold less than a pair of Jacks, or they would probably have opened the betting. You could assume that player 5 might hold at least a pair of Jacks or Queens.**

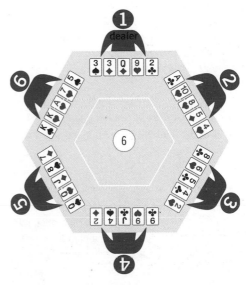

THE DEAL Player 6's betting in this hand will depend largely on the bets of the preceding players.

He could hold a pair of Aces or better, but as you hold an Ace and a pair of Kings you can take a view for now that if he holds a pair, it is probably no better than Queens (the number of cards he draws will indicate if he has better than a pair). With your pair of Kings, and with only the dealer to speak, you think you have a good chance of holding the best hand currently held. What to do? Obviously you will not fold, but should you call or raise? There is a good case here to raise.

If the Kings are the best hand, you do not want several players staying in the game and drawing, and possibly beating your hand. For example, if you call, and player 4 calls, (irrespective of what players 1, 2 and 3 might do) and players 4 and 5 stay in with you for the draw, player 4 might well draw another 9 or a second pair, and take the pot. On the other hand if you raise, you would probably force player 4 into folding, leaving you perhaps with one opponent for the pot. So you call and raise by putting in two chips, the pot now being nine chips.

4 Player 1, the dealer, faced with a bet and a raise, decides his pair of 3s is not worth risking two chips with and folds. Your strategy is working, because had he stayed in he might have drawn a third 3.

SECOND BETTING ROUND

1 Player 2 folds (he would need to draw an Ace to have much chance, and it is not worth the bet).

2 Player 3 decides to stay in and draw one card to his 8, 6, 5, 4, hoping to draw a 7 to complete a straight which, were he successful, would probably win the hand. (Note: he could also have discarded the 8, hoping to draw a 3.) To call costs him two chips, raising the pot to 11 chips. Notice that when player 3 makes his decision to call, there are nine chips in the pot, for which he risks two more chips to get

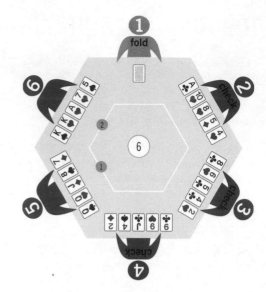

1ST BETTING ROUND   Player 6's strategy of raising player 5's bet has scared off player 1.

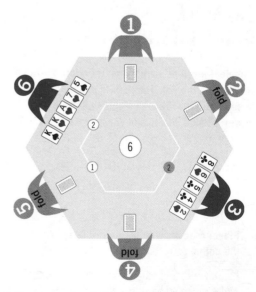

2ND BETTING ROUND   In this round, players 2, 4 and 5 all fold, while player 3 thinks his possible straight is worth staying in for.

his straight. If he is successful he wins nine (odds of 9 to 2), but we know the real odds of him converting to a straight are nearly 11 to 1, so this is a sucker bet.

3 Player 4 now folds, because with three players still in his pair of 9s is too weak to bet on.

4 Player 5, having opened the betting on a pair of Queens, also decides to fold, assuming that you probably hold something like a pair of Aces or better, and that player 3 also has a hand worth betting.

As all bets are equalized, the first betting interval now ends and you (player 6) have one rival, player 3, for a pot currently standing at 11 chips.

the draw

1 The dealer asks player 3 (the nearest active player to his left) how many cards he wants. Player 3 discards his ♥2 and draws one card.

2 It is now your turn to decide how many cards to draw, and you have to decide whether to draw three to your pair of Kings, or to keep the Kings with the Ace as a kicker and draw two cards. It is probably better to draw three cards. You must assume that player 3 is drawing one card to try to fill a straight or a flush. Were he drawing one card to two pairs, he would undoubtedly have opened the betting himself. If he fills to a straight or a flush he will almost certainly win, your only chance of beating him being to obtain a full house or four of a kind. In this case the better chance is to draw three, however long the odds against you. Let us assume you do not improve, and that a pair of Kings remains your hand after the draw.

second betting interval

As you are the first player who remains in the game to the left of the opening better (player 5 who has now folded), it is your place to speak first on the second betting interval.

1 Check. There is no point in doing anything else. If player 3 has filled his straight, he will win, and there is no point in giving him any more chips. If he has failed, he will fold anyway, as it would be foolish to venture any more chips on a certain loser.

As the odds were so long against player 3 drawing a 7 to fill his straight, let us assume that justice was done and he failed. The two hands after the draw are as follows:

> Player 3: ♣Q, ♣8, ♥6, ♣5, ♣4
>
> Player 6: ♠K ♥K, ♥5, ♦4, ♠2

2 After you check, Player 3 will check also, as it doesn't cost him anything, but he might as well just throw in his cards, as Queen high is not going to win anything.

showdown

The two hands are shown, and you collect 11 chips, a profit of eight chips (counting one of those in the ante as yours).

Your bold decision to raise with your pair of Kings paid off handsomely. Had you merely called in the first betting interval, player 5 and even, for the cost of a single chip, player 4 might have remained in for the draw, and if player 4 had picked up a 9 or player 5 a Queen, or indeed if either of them had collected a second pair, you would have lost.

general strategies

There are lots of sayings or beliefs of old poker players, and a couple are worth emphasizing here, since there is logic and truth behind them.

do not throw good money after bad

It is hard for a player who has a good hand and has bet accordingly, and thus contributed several chips to the pot, to come to terms with the knowledge that he is probably beaten and that to bet on would only lose even more chips. It is no good thinking, 'I've put 20 chips into this pot – I'm not going to give up now. I must risk just a few more to protect my investment.' The point to realize here is that the chips you've put into the pot do not belong to you any more; they belong to the pot.

A bet is a good bet or a bad bet according to its prospects of being a winning bet and the amount it stands to win. A 3 to 1 chance that will win you six times your stake is a good bet, a 6 to 1 chance that will win you three times your stake is a bad bet – and neither fact is influenced at all by how much of the winnings (i.e. the pot) was originally yours to begin with.

do not bet against a one-card draw

Assume you are holding three of a kind, and you are in a second betting interval with one other player who drew one card. It is your turn to speak first. The assumption is that your opponent's four cards were two pairs, in which case he might have drawn to a full house, or that he was drawing to fill a flush or a straight. In each case, the chances are, as Table 10 (pages 50–51) shows, that he will have failed, and that you hold the better hand. On the other hand, if, against the odds, he succeeded in improving his hand, he has got you beaten.

Whatever his fate in the draw, there is no point in you betting. You should check and wait to see what he does. If you bet, and he has failed to fill a straight or a flush, his hand is worthless and he will fold, so you will not win any extra chips from him. On the other hand you risk losing some, because if he has filled a straight or a flush, he will raise, and you will lose. So leave it to him. If he bets, call – you can be no worse off than if you'd bet in the first place. The only way you can lose out against him is if he fails to improve two pairs, and checks rather than bets. You will win the pot, but could have won an extra chip or two had you bet and he had been silly enough to call.

dealing with two pairs

In fact a hand of two pairs is a classic one in poker – one of the most awkward to deal with. Table 4 (page 44) shows that it is likely to be the best hand at the table after the deal, even with as many as eight players in the deal. The trouble with two pairs is that the odds are more than 10 to 1 against improvement by drawing a single card, and while it may be the best hand before the draw, it seldom is afterwards.

In fact poker players have calculated that if, after the draw, you hold a hand of two pairs you have the chances of winning shown in Table 12.

With more than three opponents remaining your chances of winning get progressively worse.

strategy

Your strategy with two pairs at the deal will partly depend on where you are sitting. Suppose one player before you has bet, and there are three or four players yet to speak. On the assumption that your two pairs represent the best hand at the table, but might not remain so, your strategy should be to try to force out the remaining players, so you raise. If they all fold, you have a good chance of taking the pot, whereas if two or three of them stay in with middling pairs, say, the chances of you taking the pot have diminished. In fact many players fear holding two small pairs and if two players bet against them after the draw, will ditch them immediately.

TABLE 12: Odds of winning holding two pairs after the draw	
Number of opponents still in	Odds of winning
one	3 to 1 on
two	slightly better than even
three	6 to 4 against

bluffing

Much is said in poker literature about bluffing, and it is easy to come to the conclusion that bluffing is the most important element of the game. Certainly poker is a game of skill rather than luck, because a good player will win consistently, and he cannot always be lucky enough to be dealt the best cards. So where is the skill? Is it from mathematical superiority, psychological superiority, or a combination of both? The answer is that the best players need both these assets.

We have dealt already with the numerical aspects of poker, of hands in terms of their likelihood, and the probabilities of improving hands in the draw, etc. and clearly the best players need a knowledge of these things. It is not necessary to carry every fact in the tables in one's head, of course, but a general instinct of what they convey is essential.

Yardley's bluff

One of the most outrageous examples of bluffing, claimed in his well-known book *The Education of a Poker Player* to have been successfully executed countless times by Herbert Yardley, relies upon a player building a reputation as a tight player, who bets only on good hands. When the time is ripe, and he is the dealer, or near to the dealer's right (i.e. one of the last to speak), and one or two players have bet, Yardley would raise, even with a hand containing not even a pair. Seeing a man who only bets with a good hand going in with a raise was calculated to encourage the players left in to fold, which they frequently did, and Yardley collected. If one or even two called, and drew cards, Yardley, speaking last, would stand pat.

This was calculated to scare further any players who remained in, who would usually do no more than check, at which Yardley would bet the maximum. This, according to Yardley, was enough, time after time, to persuade all other players (there was usually at this stage no more than one) to fold rather than to match his bet, since they were certain that he held at least a straight. In practice, of course, his hand might have been nothing better than, say, Jack high.

This bluff works best when the game is one of variable limit, pot limit or no limit, since it is the size of the bet coming from a notoriously tight player that deters the others from contesting it. In a limit game a player might be good enough to call you.

the psychology of bluffing

The psychological aspect of poker lies in the ability to study and draw inferences from the behaviour and play of the other players. Is a particular opponent a good player or a bad player? Can you deduce the strength of his hand by the giveaway signs of excitement or by the way he has played previous hands? By the same token, can you prevent him discovering from your demeanour and style of play the same things about you? Or can you lead him to draw false conclusions about you or your hand by bluffing?

It is hard to say which of the two skills, numerical or psychological, is the more important to the complete poker player. It is true that, at the showdown, only the best hand wins. But this might not necessarily be the best hand that was held during the deal. The holder of the best hand may have been bluffed into folding before the showdown.

Bluffing is to mislead other players of the value of your hand, and can be used in two ways.

1 You bet heavily to persuade opponents that you have a much better hand than you truly have so that rather than contributing chips to the pot in order to call you they fold. By this means you can win a pot with the poorest hand at the table.

2 Less spectacular but more subtle and more common, you attempt to persuade opponents that your hand is less good than it actually is, so that they stay in the deal longer and contribute more chips, which means a bigger jackpot when you eventually, as you hope, win the showdown.

The first type of bluff works best when the limits are high and to call the bluff requires risking a large number of chips. If the limits are low, an opponent will be likely to call you and your bluff will fail. The examples overleaf show the difference the limit makes – your bluff will probably fail in the first and succeed in the second.

jargon-buster

stand pat to decline to take cards at the draw. Since only hands of the value of a straight upwards cannot be improved by a draw, a player who stands pat either has picked up a straight or better at the deal, or is bluffing.

EXAMPLE
WORKING A BLUFF 1

Suppose there are six players and the ante is six chips. The limit for a bet and a raise is one chip before the draw and two chips after. In the first betting interval, you are the dealer and one player has bet one chip and another called before you.

1 You call and raise one chip.

2 The first opponent folds, the other calls. There are 11 chips in the pot before the draw.

3 You stand pat.

4 Your opponent checks and you bet two chips.

There are now 13 chips in the pot and to force a showdown your opponent needs to pay only two chips. At odds of 13 to 2, he might decide to risk his couple of chips just to make sure you aren't bluffing. If he doesn't, you take the 13 chips. Since you contributed five (including your one for ante – actually as dealer you put in the whole ante of six), you have won eight. Not bad, considering you had a completely worthless hand. But it is more likely your opponent will call and you will lose the pot.

EXAMPLE
WORKING A BLUFF 2

Suppose you are playing pot limit. Again, there are six chips in the ante.

1 The same two opponents each bet one chip.

2 You call for one chip, making nine in the pot and raise by nine chips.

3 Both opponents will probably fold. You collect 18 chips, 11 of which you put in yourself (including one for the ante). Your profit is seven chips.

However, what happens if one of your opponents, holding, say, two pairs, Aces high, calls rather than folding?

He draws one card (and fails to complete a full house – the odds are over 10 to 1) and you stand pat.

4 He now checks.

5 You bet the amount in the pot, which is now 27 chips.

6 Your opponent now has to put 27 chips into the pot to call you. You have stood pat, and you are a tight player. He must assume you have a straight at least. With his two pairs is he going to put another 27 chips into the pot to see your hand? Probably not. He will fold.

7 You collect a pot of 54 chips, 38 of which you contributed yourself. You make a profit of 16 chips. Of course, had your opponent called you for 27 chips, you would know the game is up. He probably has a full house.

bluffing with a good hand

Bluffing when holding a poor hand is very difficult in Draw Poker when there are limits. Without limits, or with potentially large limits, such as in pot limit, the size of the bet can force timid players to fold winning hands, but when it costs no more than a couple of chips, say, to call, most players with any sort of hand will pay the two chips rather than never know whether they have been bluffed or not, so the bluff will fail.

On the other hand, bluffing when holding a good hand, in order to entice more chips into the pot, is a strong weapon in the hands of a good player.

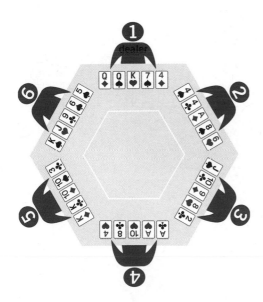

AFTER THE DEAL

EXAMPLE
CALLING A BLUFF

In the hand shown to the left, the limit, bet or raise, is one chip before the draw, two afterwards. The pot is six chips. Player 1 is the dealer.

first betting interval

FIRST BETTING ROUND

1 **Player 2 speaks first. With a small pair and an Ace kicker he checks.**

2 **Player 3, with a prospect of a straight, bets one.**

3 **Player 4, with a pair of Aces, calls.**

4 **Player 5, with two pairs, calls and raises one.**

5 **Player 6, King high, folds.**

6 **The dealer, with three players betting, decides to fold his pair of Queens.**

SECOND BETTING ROUND

1 Player 2 decides that the idea of drawing two cards to his pair of 4s and a kicker is not a good one and folds also.

2 Player 3 calls, adding another chip to the pot.

3 Player 4, reasoning that at least he knows he has the highest pair among the hands, and because it will cost him only one chip to stay in for the draw, also calls, putting his chip into the pot.

The first betting interval is over, with players 3, 4 and 5 still in, and 12 chips in the pot.

the draw

1 Player 3, being the nearest active player to the dealer's left, draws first, and draws one, discarding ♣2. He draws ♣7 and completes his straight.

2 Player 4 draws next and discards ♥10, ♣8 and ♥4, drawing ♥7, ♦7 and ♠9. He now holds two pairs, Aces up.

3 Player 5 discards ♣3 and draws ♦6 – he has not improved.

second betting interval

FIRST BETTING ROUND

1 Player 3, who was the first to bet in the previous betting round, has completed his straight, but with two other players in, he decides to bluff, and checks.

2 Player 4 knows that his hand, with Aces up, would be the highest if all hands were of two pairs, which he suspects is the case, as both players 3 and 5 drew one card. His view is that both drew to two pairs, and that as the odds are more than 10 to 1 against improving two pairs, he might well now hold the best hand. He reasons that player 3, who merely checked, has not improved his hand. He decides to bet two chips.

3 Player 5 is in a spot as he thinks player 4 might have improved to three of a kind. However, he reasons that player 4, on the other hand, might have improved only to two pairs, and since he drew three cards and was thus not retaining an Ace kicker, player 4's two pairs would not match his own two pairs of Kings high. He, too, reasons that player 3 probably has not improved on two pairs, and with his Kings and 10s, he considers it worth two chips to call.

SECOND BETTING ROUND

1 Player 3 likes his Jack-high straight and now calls two and raises two, adding four chips to the pot.

2 Player 4, now throwing good money after bad, calls.

3 Player 5 folds.

showdown

Player 3 wins with his straight, and collects a pot of 22 chips, a profit of 15 chips. Had he not bluffed and, instead of checking in the second betting interval, had bet, it is likely that player 4 might have called and player 5 folded, thus reducing his profit by four chips to 11.

when and when not to bluff

Despite the value of bluffing, and psychology in general, and the fact that many top players will argue for its precedence over mathematics in poker, the fact remains that if there is a showdown, you've got to have the best hand to win the pot. Bluffing is of no use at all once the hands are exposed. Therefore you should bluff only when you can see the likelihood of a bluff being successful.

who to bluff

Sometimes it is easier to bluff a good player, who will fold when he thinks he is beaten, than a poorer player who will allow the bluff to go over his head. If you are exaggerating the value of your hand, for instance, a poor player who regularly loses money because he presses on to a showdown when he cannot win, will sometimes embarrass you by exposing your bluff. If you consistently bet when the odds are against you, just to experience the joy of occasionally winning a pot with a bluff, you will almost certainly lose over the long run.

On the whole, bluffing is likely to be more profitable in Stud Poker and Hold 'Em than in Draw Poker, and more about bluffing will be discussed then.

OTHER VERSIONS OF DRAW POKER

There are hundreds of poker variations and while most can be dismissed as tinkering about to make the game more entertaining or less monotonous, and would be dismissed out of hand by serious players, a number have proved popular over a period of time. Descriptions of the more established variations follow.

Jackpots

This must be mentioned first because it is the most popular form of Draw Poker, especially in the United States, and frequently textbooks will describe this version as poker itself, rather than a variation.

The difference from the game already described is merely that a player has to hold in the deal a hand of a pair of Jacks or better in order to open the betting. Once a player has opened, the other players can call, bet or raise as they wish.

A player who opens the betting must be able to show in due course that he held an opening hand, i.e. a hand of a pair of Jacks or better. If he folds before the showdown he must retain his hand in order to demonstrate that he had the necessary values. For this reason, he must also retain his discards at the draw because it is permissible for him to 'split his openers', i.e. to discard one or more of the cards that contributed to the combination that allowed him to open.

For example, if a player is dealt the hand below, his pair of Jacks entitles him to open the betting. When it comes to the draw, he might well decide to discard the ♣J, giving him the chance of a straight flush (with ♦10), a flush (with any other diamond) or a straight (with any other 10).

Table 10 (see pages 50–51) shows that he has roughly a 3 to 1 against chance of completing one of these hands, which might well take the pot. It is a better bet than drawing three cards to his Jacks, where the odds against him achieving a better hand than any of the above are about 75 to 1. However, if he discards the ♣J and the discard is collected up, he will have no way of proving later, whether he folds or wins the pot with a straight flush, that he held a requisite hand to open. So he must keep the discarded ♣J, face down of course.

EXAMPLE
BASIC JACKPOTS HAND

There are five players, with the dealer placing five chips in the pot as the ante and with a limit of two chips to bet or raise before the draw and five chips after the draw.

first betting interval

FIRST BETTING ROUND

1 **Player 1 is dealer, so player 2 is first to speak. He holds a four-card straight, open at both ends, but hasn't the necessary hand to open.**

2 **Player 3 holds a four-card flush, but also cannot open.**

3 **Player 4 cannot open with a pair of 10s, and neither can player 5 with a pair of 6s. All of these players check.**

4 **The dealer, with his two pairs, opens with two chips, to the relief of players 2 and 3, with their chances of a good hand. He would have been able to open with two pairs, even if the higher pair had not been Jacks or above, since a hand of two pairs is clearly higher than the pair of Jacks required to open.**

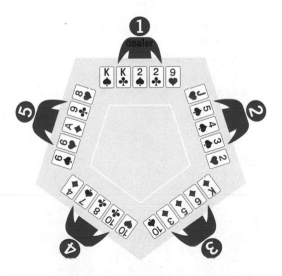

1ST BETTING ROUND Only player 1 can open the betting, even though other players hold good hands.

SECOND BETTING ROUND

1 **Players 2 and 3 call.**

2 **Players 4 and 5 fold. They know that player 1 has them beaten. Player 5 could have called, and drawn two cards to his pair, keeping the Ace as kicker, in the hope of drawing a third 6 or another Ace and winning the pot with three of a kind or two pairs Aces up, but prudently folds.**

the draw

1 **Player 2 discards ♥J, and receives ♣6, completing a straight.**

2 **Player 3 discards ♠10 and draws ♦10, completing a flush (there could be fireworks ahead).**

3 **The dealer discards ♥9 and draws ♥5.**

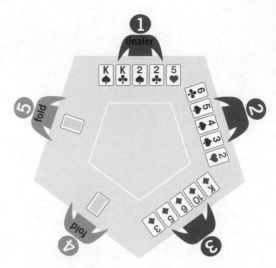

AFTER THE DRAW Players 2 and 3 have improved their hands in the draw, while player 1 has not.

---

deal passed out 1

If no-one has two Jacks or better, the deal is 'passed out'. The deal now passes to the next player, with the rules remaining the same. There is another ante (in this case the new dealer adds another five chips to the pot, making the ante ten) and the cards, after the shuffle and cut, are redealt. If the deal is passed out again, it continues round the table, with the ante increasing each time. It would be rare, of course, for more than two or three deals to be passed out consecutively. A pair of Jacks or better should appear approximately once in five hands, so with five players the odds against getting a run of three passed out hands are about 7 to 1 against and, with more than five they are over 60 to 1 against.

deal passed out 2

Rather than redealing the cards if nobody is able to open, an alternative is for all players to keep their hands and play then as Lowball (see page 75).

second betting interval

FIRST BETTING ROUND

1 It is dealer's turn to speak first, as the first to bet. He checks (if one or both of his opponents have filled to a straight or a flush, they will doubtless bet, and eventually beat him, so there's no point in contributing any more to their winnings).

2 Player 2 is not interested in everybody checking as he holds a good hand and he bets the maximum of five chips.

3 Player 3 realizes that player 2 could have filled to a straight, a flush or a full house, the last of which would beat him, but reckons that if he cannot raise with a King flush he never will, and calls five and raises five.

SECOND BETTING ROUND

1 Player 1 now folds, his two pairs almost certainly beaten, but keeps his hand because he must show his pair of Kings gave him the right to open.

2 Player 2 thinks his small run is probably beaten, but being a player who thinks it worth five chips to be absolutely sure (he hates the notion of being bluffed), he calls.

showdown

Player 3 wins. He takes the pot of 31 chips, a profit of 18 chips.

If, at the showdown, the opener cannot show that he possessed the required opening cards, the penalties are as follows.

- If the opener is involved in the showdown, he cannot win the pot and his hand is dead. If there is only one other player in the showdown, he takes the pot. If there is more than one, then the player with the best hand wins.

- If the opener bet and was not called, his bet is forfeited and remains in the pot for the next deal.

- If the opener bet and other players called and then folded, so that only the opener remained, all the money in the pot is returned to the players who made bets, the opener's bets remaining forfeit in the pot.

- If during the first betting interval, the opener announces that he lacked the cards to open before all bets are equalized, all other players withdraw their chips from the pot, except the ante. The opener's chips remain in the pot. Players in turn from the opener's left may open if they have the right cards.

- If one of the other players bets, the false opener may remain in by calling or raising but must put new chips into the pot – those he contributed earlier are forfeited.

- If no player after the false opener wishes to open, then the deal moves to the next player in turn, with the false opener's chips remaining in the pot for the following deal.

Progressive Jackpots

Progressive Jackpots is played exactly like Jackpots until a deal is passed out. While the deal still passes to the next player, and the ante is repeated, the next deal becomes Queenpots, wherein a pair of Queens or better is required to open the betting. Should the deal be passed out again, a pair of Kings is required, and if this is not achieved, the next deal requires a pair of Aces. After Aces, the requirement to open drops – it goes to Kings, then Queens, then Jacks, then back to Queens, Kings, Aces and so on back and forth.

Spit in the Ocean

There are many variations of Spit in the Ocean. The distinguishing feature of the game is that the players are dealt four cards each face down, and a final card is then placed face up in the centre of the table. This card is the spit, and it is regarded as the fifth card in each players' hand.

However, this card, and the three others in the pack of the same rank, is regarded as a 'wild' card (see pages 34–35). This means that each player can regard the spit as whatever card he wishes. For example, a player who is dealt ♣A, ♣K, ♣J and ♣10, in effect holds a royal flush, the highest hand in most forms of poker, because whatever the spit, he can regard it as the ♣Q.

The hands of all players in Spit in the Ocean therefore consist of the four cards dealt them, plus one wild card. However, since all cards of the rank of the spit are wild, a player might hold two wild cards in his hand, or even three.

It is vital in games of spit for the players to agree beforehand how wild cards are to be evaluated. The general rule is that a wild card can't be used to duplicate a card already held in the hand, thus a hand of five of a kind would be impossible. In the absence of official rules for the game, this is recommended as best procedure. However, there are players who prefer to allow a hand of five of a kind and other hands that are impossible without wild cards (see page 35).

Players ante before the deal as usual. There is usually only one betting interval. First to speak is the player on the dealer's left, and he has the same options as in the standard form of Draw Poker, i.e. initially to check or bet, and after betting commences to call or raise or fold. When bets are equalized, the showdown takes place.

EXAMPLE
SPIT IN THE OCEAN HAND

The ♦5 in the centre of the table is the spit. Player 1 is dealer, there are five chips in the pot and it costs two chips to bet, with a maximum raise of five.

betting interval

FIRST BETTING ROUND

1　Player 2 is in the lucky position of holding a second wild card as his ♣5 is the same rank as the spit. Nevertheless the best hand he can make is an A, K, Q, J, 10 straight, not a bad hand but one not guaranteed to win at Spit in the Ocean. He decides to bet the minimum of two chips and await events.

2　Player 3 has three of a kind (8s). It is not the worst hand he could have, but he decides it is not unlikely that somebody will be able to do better than three 8s and folds.

3　Player 4 also has a second wild card, and has been dealt two Aces, so his hand is four Aces, almost an unbeatable hand in any form of poker, and a powerful one even in Spit in the Ocean, so he calls the two and raises by the maximum of five chips, hoping that somebody might call.

4　Player 5 also has an excellent hand, since with the wild card he can make a full house, beatable only by four of a kind or a straight flush. It costs him seven chips to stay in the game, but he calls.

SECOND BETTING ROUND

1　Player 1, the last to speak as dealer, can use the wild card as an 8, and complete a straight, but in view of the level of betting so far wisely decides to fold.

2　Player 2 now has the difficult choice of whether to fold, call or raise with the highest straight. There are 21 chips in the pot and he

AFTER THE DEAL　The ♦5 wild-card spit strengthens the hands of players 2 and 4 as they both hold 5s.

needs to put in five more in order to share a three-way showdown. The odds offered are just over 4 to 1. It is certainly not worth raising, he thinks. He can beat any other straight and three of a kind but anybody who has filled to a flush or better has him beaten. Reluctantly, but as it turns out wisely, he folds.

3　There is a showdown, and player 4 wins with his four Aces, a profit of 13 chips.

As a matter of strategy it is interesting to consider what might have happened had he merely called on his first bet. Possibly no other players would have raised, in which case he would have five fewer chips. But suppose player 5, with his full house, had raised, as is probable, even by the minimum of two. Player 2 would probably have called for another 2, and then player 4 could have raised by five. If player 5 called, the pot would then be 27 chips, a profit of 17 to player 4.

variations on Spit in the Ocean

VARIATION 1

A draw element can be added. After a deal as described above, there is a draw, in which players can discard any of the four cards of their hands as dealt, and replace them with new cards dealt by the dealer. There is then a second betting interval, with the first player to bet previously being the first to speak. When bets are equalized, there is a showdown.

VARIATION 2

There are five betting intervals. One card is dealt face down to each player, after which there is a betting interval. After the second, then the third, then the fourth cards are dealt face down to each player, there is a corresponding second, third and fourth betting interval. Then the spit is dealt face up on the table as before and becomes the fifth card of each players' hand. As before, it, and other cards of its rank, are wild. There is then a fifth betting interval, followed by the showdown.

VARIATION 3 – WITHOUT WILD CARDS

This is played exactly as the game outlined above, but the spit, while still being the fifth card of all players' hands, is not wild, and nor are the other cards of its rank. Note that in the deal on the previous page, player 4 would still have the best hand with two pairs, Aces up. He would beat player 5's hand, which is not helped by the spit and remains two pairs, Kings up. Player 2 is the only other player helped by the spit, but only to a pair of 5s. If the object of playing Spit in the Ocean is to make outstanding hands like straight flushes and full houses more common, then it is pointless to play it without the spit being wild.

VARIATION 4 – THE WILD WIDOW

This is a more interesting variation. The cards are dealt as above, i.e. four face down to each player, followed by the spit face up in the centre of the table. However this time the spit is not part of any players' hand. Its purpose is to denote that the other three cards of its rank are wild.

During the first betting interval each player knows the identity of only four cards of his final hand, i.e. those four dealt face down to him. However, he knows if he has any wild cards, and can assess the possible values of his hand in respect of how it might be improved by his fifth card, which is dealt after the first betting interval. When all bets are equalized, this fifth card is then dealt face down to each player and the second betting interval takes place.

Of course it is quite possible that a player's fifth card could be a wild card, so the betting can be interesting and speculative, with the fifth card being likely to change everybody's fortunes.

Lowball, or Low Poker

Lowball is played in the same way as Straight Draw Poker, with no minimum requirement needed to open, but with one great difference, the lowest hand wins. However, the ranking of the cards is simpler:

- flushes and straights are ignored.

- Ace counts low in all respects. Thus the lowest hand that can be held is, 5, 4, 3, 2, A – the five lowest cards in the pack. It is known as a 'bicycle'. As straights are ignored, it doesn't count as a straight, and if all the cards were of the same suit, it wouldn't count as a flush either.

As between unmatched hands (i.e. those not containing a pair, triple or four), the highest-ranking card determines the order, and if equal the next highest.

- 10, 7, 6, 5, A beats 10, 8, 3, 2, A by virtue of the 7 being lower than the 8.

The same applies to pairs:

- 8, 8, K, 5, 2 loses to 7, 7, K, 5, 2 and loses to 8, 8, 10, 9, 6, but beats 8, 8, K, 6, A.

Table 13 (overleaf) shows the ranking of some hands in lowball.

The procedure is as in Straight Draw Poker, with the first and second betting intervals, and a showdown.

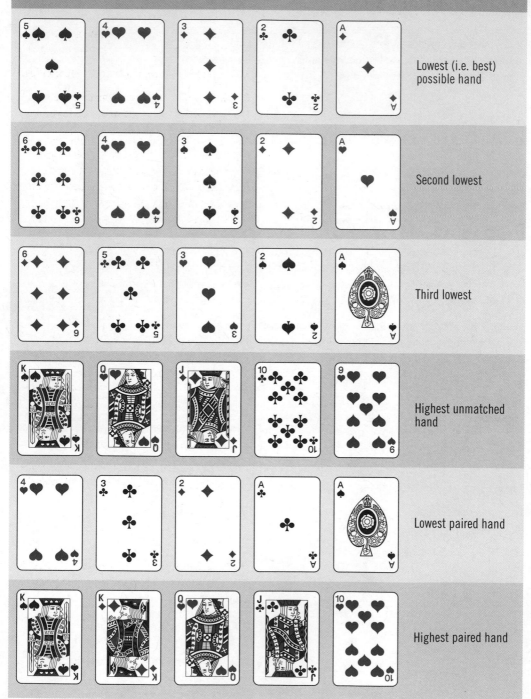

Lowest (i.e. best) possible hand

Second lowest

Third lowest

Highest unmatched hand

Lowest paired hand

Highest paired hand

EXAMPLE
BASIC LOWBALL HAND

Limits to bet and raise are two chips before the draw and five afterwards. The ante is six chips.

AFTER THE DEAL Only player 5 has a really promising hand; 2, 3 and 4 have middling hands, and the hands of players 1 and 6 are very poor for Lowball.

first betting interval

FIRST BETTING ROUND

1 **Player 2 speaks first and checks, as do players 3 and 4.**

2 **Player 5, with a promising hand, bets 2 chips.**

3 **Player 6, with a hand from which he would have to discard two Jacks and an 8, folds.**

4 **Player 1, the dealer, would have to discard a 6, plus the two big cards, King and 10, so he folds, too. Generally, in Lowball, to have to draw more than one card means the hand is not too good – if it is necessary to draw three, it is best to fold straight away.**

SECOND BETTING ROUND

1 **Player 2, who checked, could discard a 9 and hope for an Ace, 3, 4, 6 or 8 to give him a hand of 9 high, but 9 high is not brilliant and he is a tight player so he folds.**

2 **Player 3 goes to the other extreme. Only one player has bet, and there is only one to come so he takes the optimistic view and calls, intending to discard Q, 5 and hoping to draw two small cards from 2, 3, 4, 6 or 7.**

3 **Player 4 is in a similar position – he must drop K, 7 and hope for an 8-high hand. He calls too.**

The first betting interval is over with 12 chips in the pot and players 3, 4 and 5 still in, with player 5 a firm favourite.

the draw

1 **Player 3 draws two cards, and gets 10, Ace for his Queen, 5, leaving him with the lowest pair, Aces.**

2 **Player 4 draws 2, 2, for his K, 7 and finishes with a pair of 2s.**

3 **Player 5 discards a 4 and receives a King, leaving him King high.**

second betting interval

Player 5 is faced with a difficult choice. He now has a poor hand, King high. In practice, in Lowball, unmatched hands are usually announced by naming the highest two cards, so he would think of his hand as King, 7. However, both his opponents drew two cards and quite easily could have found a pair or picked up a high card themselves (none higher than King, unfortunately for him). But from his point of view it is conceivable that each opponent could be something like Queen or 10 high, whereas from their point of view player 5 could have a very good hand, having drawn only one card. It is a perfect situation for a bluff.

1 Player 5 bets the maximum of five chips. If raised, he would probably fold.

2 Because players 3 and 4 have picked up pairs they both fold immediately.

Player 5 takes the pot of 17 chips, a profit to him of nine chips. King, 7 would not be a hand to win many deals of Lowball.

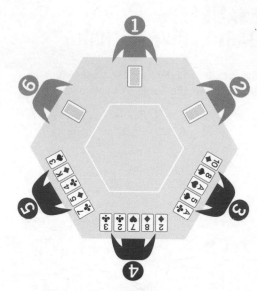

2ND BETTING INTERVAL Player 5, who bet first, actually holds a poor hand, but as he is the only player to draw one card, he decides to bluff with a maximum bet. Players 3 and 4 fold, so he wins. Ironically, he held the best hand anyway.

variations on Lowball

VARIATION 1

Lowball is sometimes played with the hands ranked in the standard manner, with Aces high and flushes and straights recognized. Thus the lowest possible hand becomes 7, 5, 4, 3, 2. Although Aces are high, they must be counted low in this variation of Lowball if they are part of the sequence A, 2, 3, 4, 5, which is regarded as a straight. A holder of this hand cannot call the Ace high, and therefore have a hand of Ace, 5 which would beat, for example, a pair.

VARIATION 2 – LOWBALL WITH JACKPOTS

When Jackpots are played in Draw Poker and a hand is passed out because nobody has the required value to open (see page 70), one popular arrangement is not to gather up the cards and reshuffle for a new deal, but to play a hand of Lowball instead, the player to dealer's left being the first to speak.

High-low Poker

This popular and interesting version of Draw Poker is played as a combination of standard poker, in which the highest-ranked hand at the showdown wins, and Lowball, in which the lowest wins. Each player has the option of playing for highest hand, lowest hand or high-low (it is possible, as we shall see, for a hand to be highest and lowest, although it is more likely in Seven-card Stud, High-low, as described in the Stud Poker section).

During the betting intervals, players do not know who is betting hoping to win the high hand and who is betting hoping to win the low. This is declared only at the showdown. At the showdown, the pot is divided equally between the player who wins high and the player who wins low. If there is an odd chip, it goes to the high player.

High hands are ranked as in standard poker, and low hands as in standard Lowball. This is where the possibility arises that a hand can be high and low. For example ♥A, ♥8, ♥5, ♥3, ♥2 could be the highest hand, ranking as an Ace-high flush, but it could also be the lowest, as in Lowball (see above) flushes are not recognized and Ace counts low, so the hand in Lowball is 8, 5 high, an excellent hand. Similarly a straight, 6, 5, 4, 3, 2 could be high and low – but this is very rare in five-card Draw Poker.

At the showdown, players must declare simultaneously whether they are competing for high, low or high-low. The commonest way to do this is for the players to secrete a chip in their hands under the table, say red for high, white for low, and one of each colour for high-low.

- If in a showdown between two players one player is competing for high and one for low, they automatically share the pot.

- If two players are competing for high and one for low, the player competing for low automatically takes the pot for low – the other two players must show their hands, the higher taking the pot for high.

- If a player competes for high-low, he must beat both high and low players – if his hand isn't high and low, he loses, and the pot is divided among the other players as if he hadn't bet. This is to say that if a player declares high-low and holds the highest hand but not the lowest (or vice versa), he loses both. The lowest hand takes the low pot and the highest hand among those left takes the high.

EXAMPLE
BASIC HIGH-LOW HAND

The ante is six chips and the limit, bet or raise, is two before the draw and five after.

first betting interval

1 Player 2 speaks first and bets two chips. He is thinking of drawing three to his Aces for high. He could go low by drawing two to A, 4, 2, but likes his Aces.

2 Player 3 calls. He is going high, too, drawing to a pair and an Ace kicker.

3 Player 4 calls. His idea is to ditch a 2, and hope for an Ace, 3 or 5 to give him a good low hand.

4 Player 5 calls. He is going low and will stand pat on 8, 7.

5 Player 6 calls. He will ditch his King and hope to complete a straight for high.

6 Player 1, the dealer, doesn't think much of his hand at all with all this activity, and cannot fold fast enough.

THE DRAW

At the draw the pot is 16 chips, with five still in.

1 Player 2 discards his 10, 4 and 2 and picks up a pair of 6s and another 10.

2 Player 3 receives a 3 and 9 in return for his Queen and 8.

3 Player 4 discards one of his 2s, getting a 5 in return.

4 Player 5 stands pat.

5 Player 6 receives a second Jack for his King.

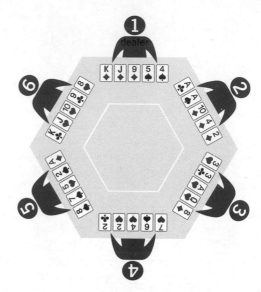

AFTER THE DEAL   Only player 1 has an obviously poor hand – the others all have chances for improvement.

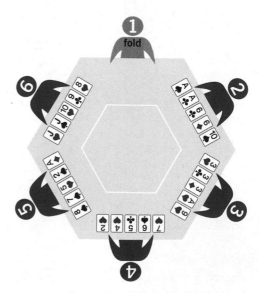

AFTER THE DRAW   The four players who drew all improved their hands.

second betting interval

FIRST BETTING ROUND

1 Player 2 has improved to two pairs, Aces up. He checks.

2 Player 3, who might well have folded on the first round, has improved to three of a kind, and decides to bet two chips.

3 Player 4 has a very good hand for low and calls two and raises five (he is hoping that some of the high and low bidders will stay in and boost what he hopes will be his pot).

4 Player 5, who stood pat, decides to call seven and raise five more. Like player 4, he does not fear players 2 and 3, as their draws of two and three cards suggest they are going high.

5 Player 6, who improved to a pair of Jacks but failed to fill his straight, folds.

SECOND BETTING ROUND

1 Player 2, requiring 12 chips to call, and holding two pairs, folds.

2 Player 3 fears that player 4 or player 5 might hold a straight or a flush to beat him for high, but in the hope they are going for low, he puts in ten chips to call.

3 Player 4 feels confident enough to raise again, putting in ten chips.

4 Player 5 now calls for five.

THIRD BETTING ROUND

1 Player 3, with relief, also calls. Had player 5 raised again, he might well have folded.

showdown

The showdown is reached with the pot standing at 67 chips. The three players select chips of each colour and under cover of the table put a chip of the required colour in one hand and place the fist containing that chip on the table. Simultaneously they reveal its colour.

- Player 3 shows a red chip, and is delighted when the other two players show white. Player 3, with his triple of 3s, collects half the pot, 34 chips (he has the odd chip), for highest hand. The other two players expose theirs.

- Player 4 announces 7, 6 while player 5 states only 8, 7. Player 4 takes the other 33 chips for low. Each has put in 20 chips (including the ante), so player 3 won 14 and player 4 won 13.

- Player 5, dealt the pat hand, is the big loser, forfeiting 20 chips. Players 2 and 6 have lost three chips each, and player 1, who didn't bet, only his ante of one chip.

Although this might not be a typical hand, it shows why High-low is popular. There is plenty of action. If at the showdown all players still in go for high and none for low, then the highest hand takes all the pot. This presents the interesting situation whereby a player who all game has been going for high might find himself in the showdown with one other player who he feels has got a higher hand. He could therefore elect to go low, and share the pot. Of course if he is wrong, and his hand is higher, it would be a hard mistake to overcome as he could have had all the pot.

Whiskey Poker

This is a form of poker derived from an older game called Commerce (and can be spelled Whisky if Scotch is preferred to Irish or Bourbon).

As in Draw Poker, each player antes one chip into the pot and receives five cards face down from the dealer. However, the hand before the dealer's is an extra hand played to the centre of the table, i.e. if there are six players, the dealer deals seven hands. This extra hand is called the widow.

Each player looks at his hand, then the player on the dealer's left decides whether to take the widow, knock, or pass.

- If he takes the widow, he places his dealt hand face up on the table and the widow becomes his hand.

- If he passes, the next player in rotation has the same options and so on so long as successive players pass.

- If he, or another player in his turn, knocks (also called closes, and usually signified by knocking with the knuckles on the table) the widow is immediately exposed.

- If nobody on the first round exchanges for the widow, the dealer exposes the widow.

jargon-buster

widow an extra hand, which in some card games can be swapped, whole or in part, for a player's hand (as in Whiskey Poker).

face card (a) a card containing a picture of a face, i.e. King, Queen or Jack. Also called a court card or picture card, for obvious reasons. (b) A card dealt face up, i.e. with its rank and suit showing, as opposed to one dealt face down.

Once the hand on the table is exposed, either by being exchanged for the widow, or by the dealer or a player knocking, each player has four options:

- He can exchange his whole hand for the widow.

- He can exchange one card from his hand for one card from the widow.

- He can pass (but he is not allowed to pass in consecutive turns).

- He can knock. He can knock in the same turn as making an exchange.

The knock on this occasion (i.e. once the hand on the table is exposed) is a demand for a showdown. After the knock, all players in turn, but not including the knocker, have the opportunity to exchange their whole hand or a card.

Once that round is completed, there is a showdown.

There are no betting intervals in Whiskey Poker, which takes away one of the distinctive features of standard poker. The hands at the showdown are valued in the usual manner and the best poker hand wins. The winner usually takes the ante, but there are two variations in the way the winner can collect:

1 There is no ante, and the lowest hand in the showdown pays the winner an agreed amount, which is usually a number of chips to match the number of players.

2 A combination of the two methods stated, i.e. each player antes one chip and at the showdown the lowest hand doubles the pot by putting in the same number of chips, the highest hand taking the lot.

Whiskey Poker is a popular game for Dealer's Choice (see page 85).

Shotgun Poker

Shotgun Poker is a variation of Draw Poker, designed to get in more betting intervals. It is played in exactly the same way, except that after each player has received three cards only there is the first betting interval. Betting takes place in the same way as for the standard game, and when bets are equalized players who haven't folded receive their fourth cards. There is a second betting interval after which the players still in get a fifth card. Play now proceeds exactly as in Draw Poker. There is another betting interval, followed by a draw, followed by, in this case, a fourth betting interval. There is then the showdown.

This is a good form of Draw Poker for those who like betting as the hand builds up, as is common in Stud Poker.

Knock Poker

Knock Poker is a good form of poker for those who like Rummy, since it combines elements of both games. The ante is one chip from each player.

The dealer deals five cards one at a time to each player and places the remainder of the pack face down on the table as the stock, turning the top card face up and laying it by the pack to form a discard pile.

Each player, beginning with the player on dealer's left, must take either the face-up top card of the discard pile or the face-down top card from the stock into his hand and discard one card face up onto the discard pile. This can be any card from his hand, even the one he has just drawn. Play proceeds in this manner with each player trying to build up a good poker hand until any player, having drawn, knocks. He then makes his discard, and each of the other players in turn may draw and discard once.

In the showdown, the highest hand takes the pot. In many games the winner also collects bonuses from the other players for either:

1 knocking and winning without drawing a card (two chips each).

2 for special high hands: royal flush (four chips each), any other straight flush (two chips each), four of a kind (one chip each). Needless to say these are rare, but the bonuses encourage players to press on for special hands before knocking.

If the stock becomes exhausted, the discard pile is turned over to form a new stock.

Red and Black

Red and Black is played exactly like standard Draw Poker, but hands aren't valued as poker hands. Instead, each red card in the hand counts as a plus value: face cards are 10 points each, Aces one point each and other cards by their index value. All black cards count as minus by the same calculation. After five cards have been dealt, there is the usual betting interval, then the draw, then a second betting interval, then the showdown, with the hand containing the highest number of points winning the pot. Players ante, check, bet, call and raise in the normal way.

The game is best played perhaps as High-low (see High-low, page 79). Of those left in at the showdown, the player with the highest score shares the pot with the player with the lowest score. It is impossible to win high and low. The players don't announce whether they are trying for high or low, although obviously at the draw each player will have one or other in mind.

Put and Take

Put and Take is sometimes called Up and Down the River. It is a simple banking game with little to suggest that it is a poker variant at all, but it is one of those games sometimes played in Dealer's Choice (see below).

The dealer is in effect the banker. He deals five cards to each player face up. He then deals five cards to the centre, face up, one at a time. These are 'put' cards. As each card is dealt to the centre, players whose hands contain a card of matching rank put into the pot a specified number of chips (see 'settlement' below). When the five cards have been dealt, and players have put into the pot as required, the dealer collects up the five cards, puts them to one side, and deals, one by one, a second set of five cards, face up. These are the 'take' cards. Each player whose hand contains a card of matching rank, takes a specified number of chips. If all the chips previously put in are taken out, the dealer must replenish the pot.

settlement

There are three main methods of settlement.

1 For the first card turned up in the 'put' and 'take' piles, each player with a matching card puts or takes one chip. For the second card the put and take is two chips, for the third three chips, for the fourth four chips and for the fifth five chips.

2 Instead of putting and taking 1, 2, 3, 4 and 5 chips as the cards are turned, players put and take 1, 2, 4, 8 and 16 chips.

3 The put and take does not depend upon the order of the five cards turned but upon their rank. Thus a player with a King in his hand puts and takes 13 chips, a Queen 12 chips, a Jack 11 chips, an Ace one chip and other cards according to their index numbers.

In each of the above methods of settlement, a player who holds two or three cards matching a put or take card in rank, must put in or take out two or three times the required amount of chips.

Dealer's Choice

Dealer's Choice is one of the most popular forms of poker in 'social' games among friends. Each dealer can choose which form of poker will be played on his deal. It introduces variety and presents different mathematical problems from hand to hand. It is best, perhaps, when not played all evening, but intermittently.

stud poker

The main distinguishing features between Stud Poker and Draw Poker are that in Stud there is no draw and most of the cards are dealt face up.

Five-card Stud Poker

The basic game is Five-Card Stud Poker, in which there are four betting intervals. Because most of the cards are dealt face up, each player knows much more about the other players' hands than in Draw Poker, giving more scope for strategy.

Because there is no draw, it is possible to play with up to ten players, although should all ten players stay in to the showdown only two cards will not be used in the play, and 40 will be exposed. This is unlikely, of course, but nevertheless the more cards exposed the longer players might take pondering the chances of improving their hands and the game could become clumsy. The game is best with six to eight players, although it is a better game than Draw Poker if there are fewer players, and can be played with plenty of action with only two players, as the film *The Cincinnati Kid* demonstrated (see page 96).

preliminaries

As with Draw Poker, the seating, the first dealer, any special rules, the stake limits and the time limit should be agreed. The deal rotates to the left as usual.

the ante

It is not usual to have an ante in Stud Poker, but players may agree to have one if they wish.

the stakes and limits

A common way of limiting the stakes in Stud Poker is to set one chip as the low limit, and set differing upper limits, usually two chips for bets and raises during the first three betting intervals and, say, five chips for the fourth betting interval.

It is also common practice for the higher limit of five chips to come into operation as soon as any player has an 'open pair', i.e. a pair showing among his face-up cards. This could be as early as the second betting interval.

An alternative way of limiting stakes is to set upper limits of one chip in the first betting interval, two in the second, three in the third and four in the fourth, again usually with the proviso that the limit of four comes into operation as soon as a pair is showing.

Pot limits (see page 26), in which a player can bet or raise the size of the pot are also suitable for Stud Poker.

the play

1   After the shuffle and cut, the dealer deals one card face down to each player (known as the 'hole-card'), then one card face up. Each player examines his hole-card but does not reveal it. It is not shown until the showdown.

2   There is then a betting interval. The player with the highest card showing (i.e. the highest face-up card) must bet within the limits agreed. He has no option, i.e. he cannot check or fold. If two or more cards showing are of the same rank, the holder of the one nearest the dealer's left is the player who must open the betting. Thereafter, each player in turn must fold, call or raise. The betting continues round the table until all the bets of those players who haven't folded are equalized.

3   The dealer then deals a second face-up card to each player who remains in the game.

4   There is then a second betting interval. The first player to speak is the player with the highest poker combination in his face-up cards. Straights and flushes do not count for this purpose, so the highest possible combination at this stage is a pair. If more than one player holds a pair, the one with the highest pair speaks first. If there are no pairs, the person with the highest card speaks first (Ace, 2 beats King, Queen). If two or more players hold equal combinations, the player nearest the dealer's left speaks first.

On the second and subsequent betting intervals, the player to speak first may check rather than bet. Until a player has bet, subsequent players have the option to check, too. But as soon as a player bets, then subsequent players must either call or raise. When all bets are equal the betting interval ends. If during any betting interval after the first all the players check, the deal continues.

5 After the second betting interval, players are dealt a third face-up card.

6 The third betting interval begins with the player holding the highest combination (highest triple, pair or high card).

7 After that, players are dealt their last face-up card.

8 Finally there is a fourth and last betting interval.

the showdown

If all the players except one fold at any of the betting intervals, then the remaining player wins the pot. Otherwise the two or more players left in after the bets are equalized in the fourth betting interval reveal their hole-cards and the one with the best poker hand wins the pot.

dealer's obligations

The dealer has a more difficult task than in Draw Poker. He must point out who should bet first in each betting interval by pointing to the hand and saying 'King high' or 'Pair of 4s' or whatever. When dealing the third and fourth up-cards, he must also point out, as he deals the relevant card, whether it might be possible for the player to make a straight or flush. Thus, on the third up-card, if he deals ♥6 to ♣10 and ♦9 he should announce 'possible straight' and when dealing ♦J to ♦4 and ♦2 he should say 'possible flush'. He can also announce the pairs.

He should also ensure that players who fold don't reveal their hole-cards. The correct procedure when folding is to turn over the upcards and place them face down on the hole-card. One player's hole-card could be a vital card for another player and its premature display could affect the way the other player bets. It can be agreed that a player who folds without turning all his cards face down must pay a penalty to the pot, say two chips.

If the dealer makes a mistake, other players are allowed to point out the error. If the dealer makes a mistake in indicating who should speak first at any betting interval, the mistake can be pointed out and corrected, but if two players have bet or checked out of turn because of the dealer's error then the situation stands and the betting continues as normal.

EXAMPLE
FIVE-CARD STUD
BASIC HAND 1

The limits are one or two chips to open until a pair is showing or until the final betting interval when the upper limit rises to five chips. The shaded cards are the hole-cards, and these, of course, are known only to their holders.

first betting interval

1 After the first deal, player 4, holding the highest card showing, a Queen, is the first to speak, and bets one chip.

2 Player 5 calls, as he has King in the hole, better than any card showing.

3 Player 1 also calls, since he holds a pair of 3s, possibly the best hand out so far.

4 Player 2 folds by turning over his 2 and placing it face down on his hole-card. Although his hole-card equals the highest card showing, he holds it with a lowly 2 and he knows that possibly three at least of the players hold a better hand (in fact they all do).

5 Player 3 has an Ace in the hole so he calls too (he doesn't want to raise yet and scare everybody away, and, besides, player 1, who is known as a tight player, possibly holds a pair of 3s). The betting is now equalized, so the dealer deals each of the four players still in the game another card face up.

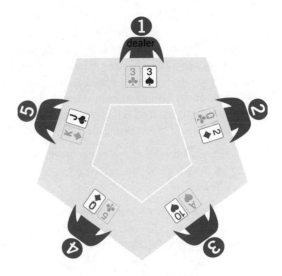

1ST BETTING INTERVAL The player with the highest up-card opens the betting – here player 4.

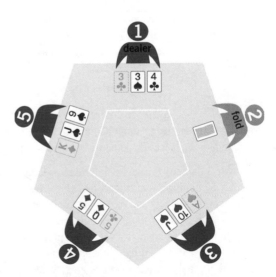

AFTER THE SECOND DEAL Apart from player 4, who now has a pair of 5s, no-one has improved his hand much.

second betting interval

1 **Player 4, with the Queen showing, is again first to bet.** He has a pair of 5s and decides to bet a chip. He still has the highest card showing and while he possibly wouldn't have stayed in without pairing his 5 he is happy to bet now and is not afraid of increasing the pot.

2 **Player 5 can still see no higher cards than his King on the table and calls,** albeit without much hope.

3 **Player 1 calls,** also without enthusiasm. He realizes his pair is unlikely to be the winning hand, but stays in for another round.

4 **Player 3 also calls.** His hand has many possibilities but he is not going to go all out yet. Once again the bets are equalized (there are now eight chips in the pot), and a further round of cards is dealt.

As the dealer deals the cards he calls 'Possible flush' for player 3, 'Pair' for player 5 and 'Possible straight' for himself. Pointing to player 5's hand, he says 'Pair of 9s to bet.'

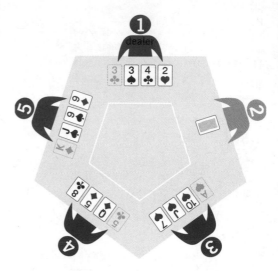

AFTER THE THIRD DEAL   Of the four players remaining in the game, players 1 and 4 will fold.

third betting interval

Because there is now an open pair on the table, the maximum limit for bets is now five chips.

1 **Player 5 decides to scare off all those without a pair by betting the maximum five chips.** He is not scared of player 1 who can hold nothing better than a pair of 4s. He will surely not stay in the hope of filling a straight or two pairs. Player 4 could have a pair of Queens, but would probably have bet more aggressively if his first two cards had been Queens. Player 3 might have paired his Jack or 10 but surely wouldn't bet on in the hope of a flush.

2 **Player 5 was right about player 1, who folds.**

3 **Player 3 knows he can beat player 5's pair of 9s if he completes a flush, or a pair of Aces, Jacks or 10s.** He is good at maths and

calculates the odds. He has seen 14 cards, including his own hole-card, and guesses that no more than two or three hearts have gone (there is only one on the table in the other hands). He reckons from the betting there are probably three Aces left in the pack and possibly two Jacks and three 10s. There are therefore about 13 cards of the 38 he doesn't know that will help him beat a pair of 9s, odds of about 2 to1 against. Of course he could also lose to two pairs in player 5's hand. The pot is currently 13 chips, offering odds of 13 to 5 against him pulling off a 2 to 1 chance. In view of his possibility of a flush, he calls.

4 **Player 4 realizes the game is up with a pair of 5s and folds.**

With bets equal, the dealer gives a final card each to players 3 and 5.

The dealer announces 'pair of 7s' when giving player 3 his card, and 'two pairs' for player 5. He says 'Two pairs bets.'

fourth betting interval

1 Player 5 knows that he has won unless player 3 has a 7 as his hole-card, which is extremely unlikely the way he has bet, so there is no need for him to do anything but check. He cannot win any more chips because player 3 must fold now that he has failed to complete a flush.

2 In the event, player 3 sees he is beaten without needing to know player 5's hole-card, and folds.

Player 5 takes a pot of 18 chips, of which 11 are profit.

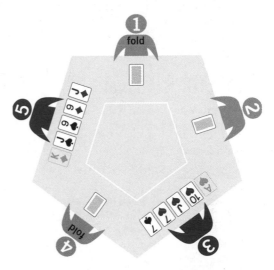

THE FINAL DEAL   Receiving the second Jack means that player 5 can be practically sure he has won.

strategy

Most players in Five-card Stud (the Poker is understood) have a general rule that it is not worth betting if there is a better hand on the table than you hold, however pregnant with possibilities your hand might be. We saw some inkling of this in the previous example when player 3 stayed in all the way with a hand that after three cards could have been a royal flush, and after four still a flush, but in the end proved to be one that had to be folded.

It follows from this rule that if on the first betting interval a player has an Ace showing and is therefore obliged to bet, all other players should fold unless they happen to have an Ace in the hole. This is reasonable mathematically, but of course if everybody followed this method very few games would ever reach a showdown, and the whole session would be a bore. So everybody loosens up a little and very frequently the first better doesn't win the pot. If you bet only when you have the best cards, you will quickly get the reputation of being such a tight player that you won't get invited to games.

EXAMPLE
FIVE-CARD STUD
BASIC HAND 2

Suppose you are player 5 with the hand shown.
Betting limits are as before.

first betting interval

1   The highest card on the table is a Jack, held
    by player 1 and he bets a chip.

2   Player 2 calls.

3   Player 3 calls.

4   Player 4 calls the bet and raises two. Why?
    He either has an 8 in the hole, making a pair,
    or an Ace, or he is bluffing. You cannot see
    another card to equal your Queen, so you call.

5   Players 1, 2 and 3 also call, to end the first
    betting interval, in which all five of you have
    contributed three chips to a healthy pot of 15
    chips. You must assume now that players 1, 2
    and 3 must all have either a pair, or an Ace or
    King in the hole, be poor players or be bluffing.

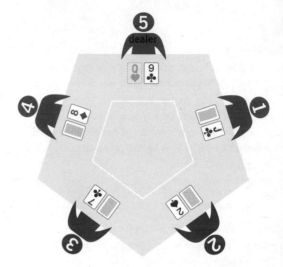

AFTER THE FIRST DEAL   Pay careful attention to other
players' bets to get clues about their hole-cards.

second betting interval

What are your options after the second deal? The
only justification for staying in would be if all
checked, indicating that none has improved, or
better still, if only player 4 bet (say two chips). You
are reckoning him for a pair of 8s. By receiving a
Queen or 9 in your last two cards (so far as you
know the remaining Queens and 9s are still in the
pack, so the odds are about 5 to 2 against), you
could be in with a shout. It would not be bad play
to raise player 4 the maximum. You would need to
put in four chips and there are already 17 in the
pot. The others might then fold on the grounds that
your 9 was paired after all. However, if any of
players 1, 2 or 3 bet again after being raised in the
first round, you should fold. To continue would
simply be throwing good money after bad.

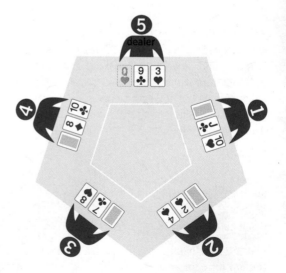

AFTER THE SECOND DEAL   With this hand you should fold,
especially if more than one opponent bets.

Five-card Stud, High-low

The procedure is as for regular Five-card Stud, with each player dealt a hole-card followed by four face-up cards, with a betting interval following each round of face-up cards. The ranks of hands are as in High-low Draw Poker (see page 79). At the showdown, players use coloured chips to declare whether they are contesting for the high or low pot.

EXAMPLE
HIGH OR LOW?

Even with four of the five cards in each hand showing, it is not always clear whether those in a showdown should call high or low.

PLAYER 1

Your hole-card is ♥J. You have a pair of Jacks. Should you call high or low? Player 2 is sure to be lower than you unless he has a straight, when he could be high and low. If he hasn't a straight, he might call low. Player 3 looks as if he could be going for low but might have a pair of Aces. Since player 2 is most likely low, you call high.

PLAYER 2

You too could be high or low. Has either player 1 or 3 completed a pair? If both, you are likely to be low; if neither, you are certainly high, with a pair of 7s. If only one has, you are unlikely to be either high or low. On the grounds that player 1 was unlikely to stay so far without a pair, you decide to call low.

PLAYER 3

You are sure you have player 1 beaten for high, but cannot beat him for low. But has player 2 a straight for high or a near-certainty for low? You doubt he has completed a straight, and go high.

Player 2 wins half the pot for low (he doesn't need to show his cards, as he is the only low), player 3 wins the other half of the pot for high, after a showdown with player 1.

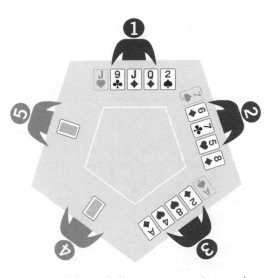

SHOWDOWN Judging whether your opponents are going high or low is vital for success at High-low Stud.

It would be very unusual for a player to hold a hand in Five-card High-low suitable for calling both high and low, but if one did, he must win both hands to win the entire pot. If he fails to win both (and a tie counts as a non-win in this case) he loses both and the pot goes to the hand or hands remaining in the showdown, according to their respective calls.

The Cincinnati Kid

The most famous hand in poker is probably the final hand of Five-Card Stud in the film *The Cincinnati Kid*. Steve McQueen, the Kid, is playing Edward G. Robinson, who is Lancey Howard, 'The Man', the champion all players want to beat.

After two up-cards, the hands are as below. It is no limit, and the pot stands at $250. The Kid, with a pair showing, is first to act, as indeed he is throughout the play of the hand. The Kid is in a strong position. He must be holding the strongest hand at the moment, because Lancey's best possible hand is a pair of 8s. The Kid bets $500, expecting to pick up the pot. From Lancey's position, he should fold. Why put another $500 into a pot for which the Kid is favourite? But Lancey not only calls the Kid, but raises him $300.

around 23–1. No poker player, certainly not 'The Man', would act as Lancey did. But he did. This is not criticism of the author of the book, Richard Jessup, of course – if Lancey had acted rationally, there wouldn't be a story at all.

The Kid immediately raises Lancey $2,000. What else would he do? Lancey must know he'd do it. He calls.

The pot now totals $5,850. This is likely to be the decisive pot of the game and The Man is playing it like a novice.

The Kid

Lancey

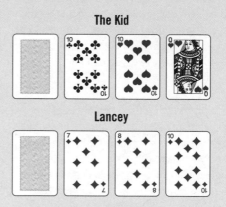

The Kid

Lancey

What is his reasoning? Well, nobody can answer that. His hole-card is ♦J, so he has chances of a flush, a straight, obviously therefore a straight flush, and of pairing his Jack to beat the Kid's two 10s. But the odds against a flush or straight are too big. To start with, he has to find a 10 for a straight, and the Kid has two of them on the table already, making the odds against Lancey getting one of the other two over 10 to 1. And then he has a nine to get. The odds against a straight are around 125 to 1. The odds against a flush are

Lancey is now dealt ♦10 (it was a 45 to 2 shot that he got ♦10 or ♦9) and the Kid ♥Q. We should now reveal the Kid's hole-card to ourselves, since it is significant. It is ♦Q, giving the Kid two pairs. When dealing Lancey's ♦10, the dealer says 'possible straight flush'.

The situation has now changed considerably, on account mainly of the 45 to 2 chance which has favoured Lancey. The Kid is still long odds on to win the hand of course. He bets $1,000.

This could be called a mistake because he has increased the pot only to $6,850, and Lancey needs to pay only $1,000 to stay in. His chances now of filling a straight or a flush, from his point of view (remember he does not know the Kid's hole-card) were 12 in 45, or under 3 to 1. His reward for pulling off this shot would be $6,850 (assuming the Kid doesn't fill to a full house). In round numbers he is being offered odds of 7 to 1 on a 3 to 1 chance, so it is now a very good bet. He calls. The pot is $7,850.

The Kid could have made it harder for Lancey by betting, say, $5,000 instead of $1,000. This would have increased the pot to $10,850 and Lancey's proposition would have looked very different – now he could win $10,850 but would need to bet $5,000. He would be getting just over 2 to 1 for his 3 to 1 chance, and even at this stage the sensible thing would be to fold.

The position after each player received his last card is highly improbable, of course, but that's the story. The Kid has completed a full house (the odds against that, knowing all the cards dealt, were nearly 14 to 1) and Lancey has completed a

The Kid

Lancey

straight flush (at odds of 43 to 1). Lancey knows he has won. The Kid thinks he has, as only the ♦6 or ♦J would be sufficient as Lancey's hole-card to beat him. On the other hand, the way Lancey has bet, the likeliest card to be his hole-card is ♦6. Anyway the Kid pushes across his last $1,400, and Lancey raises him by all he has left, too, around $4,000. The Kid writes out an IOU to call, and Lancey turns over the fateful ♦J.

An excellent story, but not one to draw useful conclusions from. Neither player played well, and if your poker career is to rely on pulling off 43 to 1 shots, you're going to be very poor, very quickly

Seven-card Stud Poker

Seven-card Stud Poker has always been more popular then Five-card in the United Kingdom, and has also become so in the United States, making it possibly the most popular form of poker for home play at the moment. The object of each player is to achieve the best poker hand using any five of the seven cards available to him.

The extra cards, both of which are known only to their holders, make for better hands and more betting, and there is more scope for better players, too. In theory the game is limited to seven players, since if all stay in to the showdown 49 cards will be in action, but it is safe to play with eight players as some players are likely to fold before the showdown.

preliminaries

The preliminaries regarding the seating, the first dealer, special rules if any, the stake limits and the playing time should all be agreed. The deal rotates to the left as usual and there are up to five betting intervals.

the ante

It is not usual to have an ante, as the betting is quite robust.

stakes and limits

It is best to have limits to the bets and raises, but what they are is a question of taste:

1 Limit each bet and raise to one or two chips.

2 Limit all bets and raises to between one and five chips.

3 Compromise and limit the first three betting intervals (by which time each player still in will have five cards) to one or two chips, and then increase the upper limit to five chips for the last two betting intervals.

The usual convention in Five-card Stud, of increasing the limit as soon as a pair is showing, is not usually bothered with in Seven-card Stud as the two hole-cards reduce the significance of the cards showing.

the deal

After the usual shuffle and cut, the dealer deals one card to each player face down, then a second face down, then a third face up. Players carefully look at their face-down cards.

the play

As with Five-card Stud, at the first betting interval the player with the highest up-card must bet, and subsequent players fold, call or raise. When all active bets are equal, a second face-up card is dealt to all still in and a second betting interval takes place. As with Five-card Stud, the highest hand showing speaks first, but now, and on subsequent rounds, he may check.

The dealer has the same obligations as in Five-card Stud, and must specify who is to speak first at each betting interval, and on the third and subsequent betting intervals should point out the possibility of flushes and straights as he deals the cards.

After the third betting interval (when each player has five cards), a sixth card is dealt, face up. There is a fourth betting interval, and then a seventh card is dealt to all players still in, but this time face down.

Players look at this last face-down card (but without revealing it to other players) and a fifth and final betting interval takes place. At this time all the players still in the deal have three face-down cards and four face up.

the showdown

If two or more players remain in the deal after the bets are equalized in the fifth betting interval, a showdown takes place. Each player exposes his three hole-cards and from the seven cards available to him forms his best poker hand. The player with the best hand takes the pot.

EXAMPLE
SEVEN-CARD STUD HAND

The stakes are limited to two chips for three rounds and five chips for the last two rounds.

first betting interval

Player 5 bets two chips and the other four players, all of whom see some encouragement in their cards, call. The pot is 10 chips.

second betting interval

1   The first to speak now is player 1, because he has a pair showing, and he bets two chips.

2   Player 2 calls.

3   Player 3 also calls.

4   Player 4 calls.

5   Player 5, however, the first to bet in the previous round, now folds with four players showing interest and a pair on the table. He holds four unrelated cards: ♠7, ♥9, ♥A and ♦4, and wisely sees no point in contesting the hand further. He turns his up cards over. Four players remain in with 18 chips in the pot.

third betting interval

After the next round of cards is dealt, the limit is now five chips, and player 1's pair is still highest.

1   He bets two chips, having three of a kind.

2   With two cards to come player 2 needs to pick up a Jack for a straight (and no Jacks have so far shown), or alternatively two spades for a flush. Although the odds are against him, the pot is big and he ventures another two chips.

3   Player 3 has two pairs, Kings up, and calls.

4   Player 4 decides to give up on to his pair of 6s and folds. The pot is 24 chips.

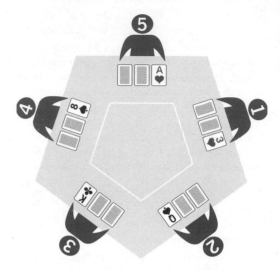

1ST BETTING INTERVAL   Player 5 will be the first to bet, since he has the highest up-card.

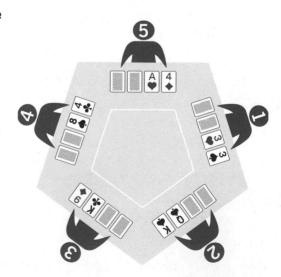

2ND BETTING INTERVAL   Player 1's pair now outranks the other hands, so he bets first.

fourth betting interval

1 **Player 1 is first to speak again, as he has two pairs showing. In fact, of course, he has a full house. He decides to bet the maximum of five chips. He knows the other hands are likely to include two pairs. He knows the other players in are likely to guess he has a full house but he would be quite happy if the others folded before the last face-down card, which might fill either of them with a full house and one likely to be bigger than his.**

2 **Player 2 realizes the game is up and is not going to throw any more money into a pot he knows he won't win. He folds.**

3 **Player 3 is in the unlikely position of holding three pairs. He knows if he can pick up a King, 9 or 5 with his final card, he will win. If he has remembered the cards he has seen face up so far, he will recall only one King, and no 9s or 5s, so he can assess exactly the odds against him. There are five cards that would win him the pot (unless player 1 has four of a kind) of the 33 cards he hasn't seen, so there are 28 that would lose him the pot. The odds against him winning are 28 to 5. He has to put in five chips to call and the pot is 29 chips – it is near enough an even bet for him. He calls. There are now 34 chips in the pot. Players 1 and 3 now receive their seventh cards face down.**

fifth betting interval

1 **Player 1 checks. If player 3 bets, he will call. Otherwise he is happy with the situation.**

2 **Player 3 also checks.**

showdown

Player 1, whose seventh card was the ♦7, shows his full house. Player 3's seventh card was the ♦2. Player 1 picks up the 34 chips.

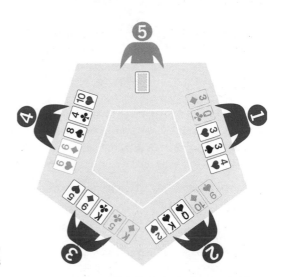

3RD BETTING INTERVAL With the hole-cards revealed to us, we see that player 1 has three of a kind, player 2 the possibility of a straight and player 3 two pairs.

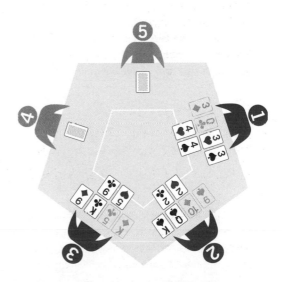

4TH BETTING INTERVAL Players 1 and 3 have strong hands, but the probability of a straight is fading for player 2.

It is unlikely that player 1 could have been bluffed out of his pot once his first four cards had provided his triple 3s. The best chance would have been when he received his sixth card to fill his full house. He raised by five chips.

Suppose player 3 had not merely called but moved in with a raise of five chips himself. Player 1 would call and they would receive their last cards with 44 chips in the pot. Player 1 would now seriously think that player 3 might hold 9, 5 or 9, K or perhaps a pair of 5s as hole-cards, completing a full house that would beat his own.

After the seventh cards, which helped neither player, and player 1 checked, suppose player 3 bet the maximum. Would the bluff work? It's unlikely. With 49 chips in the pot, player 1 had to call for five chips and player 3 would merely have lost 10 more chips than he did.

The fact is, when the pot is reasonably big, players are going to be called. Player 1 might be convinced that player 3 has a bigger full house, but he couldn't bear not knowing for sure. It is worth five chips to put his mind at rest. Only if the stakes were pot limit (see page 26), allowing player 3 to bet 44 chips on the last round, or no limit, when he might put in, say, 200 chips, is he likely to test player 1's resolve to the point where he might fold.

strategy

The first decision you must make in Seven-card Stud is probably the most important. It comes when you have to decide whether to stay in or not at the first betting interval, when you have two hole-cards and an up-card. You should visualize the sort of hand you are looking for and look at the other players' up-cards to see if any of the cards you might need are already dealt. It is necessary, of course, to have chances of a good hand – two moderate pairs are unlikely to be good enough to take the pot at Seven-card Stud. Staying in with no clear possibilities in mind, hoping that you'll get a card that might suggest a hand developing, is a sure way to contribute to a pot you'll eventually drop from.

So what constitutes a promising hand? Basically, you can consider five combinations:

1 Three of a kind. This is obviously the best possible combination, with chances of a full house or even four of a kind. Stay in, but while the betting keeps going, don't raise. Keep your secret as long as possible. Start raising later on.

2 A pair with an odd card. This should be either a big pair, say picture cards or above, or if it's smaller the odd card should be high, say Ace or King. It is important to keep track of any matching cards that get dealt to other players and spoil your chances of improving. Rarely continue beyond the fifth card without at least two pairs, and if a pair is showing higher than your best, beware.

3 Three of the same suit. You are aiming at a flush. If the fourth or fifth cards don't help, fold. Needing two of a suit from two is a long shot, even if not so many of the suit are showing.

4 Three to a straight. But if after two rounds you haven't got four consecutive cards go no farther. Beware possible straights with gaps. They are dangerous to keep, as the chances of filling them are low.

5 Two or three high cards, such as Ace, Queen, Jack or Ace, King, 6. But if the next card fails to provide a pair, fold. Four unrelated cards are unlikely to improve to anything.

The above are good rules of thumb, but keep track of other hands and combinations of cards you might hold that can be helped in more than one direction. For example, if you hold ♥A, ♥4 in the hole, and your face-up cards are ♣A, ♥5, ♥6, you hold only a pair of Aces, but you also hold chances of flush, straight, full house or even a straight flush. It's worth staying to see your next card.

betting strategy

When it comes to betting, if both your hole-cards are active in providing you with a winning hand, bet moderately at first – you want to keep the other players in and so shouldn't give away that your hole-cards are promising.

If your strength is showing (say a pair of up-card Aces) you could raise as if they completed three of a kind for you and scare off players who might if they stayed get a small triple themselves and beat you, or players who look as if they're developing a straight.

Always keep watch on opponents' up-cards and try to figure out their strengths. And however attractive your chances might look, if you are sure another player has a better hand, it's best to fold and cut your losses.

Seven-card Stud, High-low

Seven-Card Stud, High-low is one of the best poker games, guaranteed to inspire plenty of action and betting. It is played as straightforward Seven-card Stud, as outlined above, but the seven cards provide a player who contests high and low to use different hands for each call, made up from his seven cards. The hands for both high and low rank as for Draw Poker High-low (see page 79) and at the showdown players make their calls for high or low, or for both, in the same way, with different coloured chips.

EXAMPLE SEVEN-CARD STUD, HIGH-LOW HAND

Betting limits are two chips to bet or raise to the fifth card, five chips for the last two rounds.

first betting interval

1 **Player 3 shows the highest card and bets two chips (he also has a pair in the hole).**

2 **With his odd collection player 4 folds.**

3 **With a pair in the hole, player 5 calls.**

4 **With a possible flush and an Ace in the hole, player 1 calls.**

5 **With a possible straight, player 2 calls. There are eight chips in the pot. All the players still in, except player 3, who is only thinking high, are thinking both high and low at the moment.**

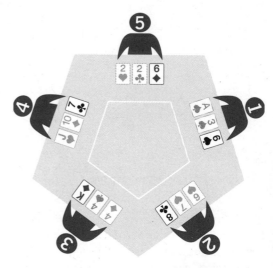

1ST BETTING INTERVAL Players 1, 2, 3 and 5 are happy to play on, but player 4 does not feel that his hand is worth pursuing.

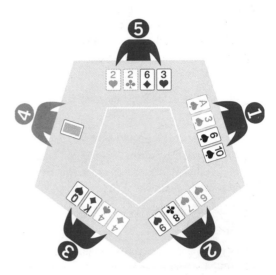

second betting interval

1 **Player 3 is still high, and bets two chips.**

2 **Player 5, with the idea of a possible low, calls.**

3 **Player 1 nearly has a flush already and calls.**

4 **Player 2's straight is progressing, and he calls. There are 16 chips in the pot.**

2ND BETTING INTERVAL The four players still in are encouraged by their hands but not so much that they bet heavily.

third betting interval

1 **Player 1 is now high with a pair of 10s. His hand is going quite well, and he bets two chips.**

2 **Player 2 likes what he sees. He could already compete for low with a complete hand at only 9 high, and with four hearts he is in line for a flush. He calls.**

3 **Player 3 decides his two 4s have taken him far enough and folds.**

4 **Player 5 seriously considers folding, but it's a friendly game and he's a loose player, so he stays in, hoping something develops – a sure recipe for disaster. There are now 22 chips at stake.**

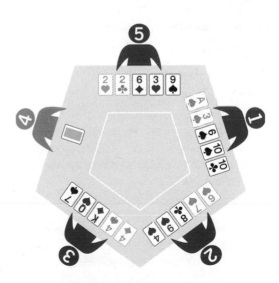

3RD BETTING INTERVAL At this point player 5 has to decide whether to play on.

fourth betting interval

1 Player 1 is high still, and with his chance of a flush and his two pairs, he bets five chips. He hopes to get rid of at least one opponent.

2 Player 2 quite likes his ♣3, and is now only 8 high for low, while a 5 or a 10 will still complete a straight, and a heart a flush. He calls five and raises five.

3 Player 5 has paid for his indecisiveness. He now folds.

4 Player 1 thinks player 2 is probably going for low, and calls his raise. There are 42 chips in the pot when the last cards of the two remaining players are dealt face down.

final deal

Player 1 gets the ♦2. It doesn't help him much. It gives him 10, 6 for low, but he doesn't think this will win. It's a pity one of his 3s wasn't a 4 – he'd have 6, 4 for low, almost unbeatable. Unless player 2 has a straight or a flush player 1 is pretty sure his own two pairs will be high, and he expects player 2 to go for low. He is going to call high.

Player 2 is delighted with events. His final card is ♥A, and he has filled an Ace flush for high and his hand for low is improved to 7 high. He decides to see what player 1 does.

fifth betting interval

1 Player 1 checks.

2 Player 2 decides to bet five chips and go for high-low.

3 Player 1 calls.

To win the pot for high-low, player 2 can provide two hands. Player 1's high hand is ♠10, ♣10, ♠3, ♦3, ♠A. Player 2 beats this with his Ace flush, and 7, 6, 4, 3, A takes low. He pockets 52 chips.

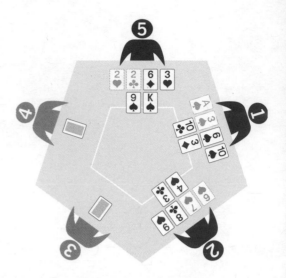

4TH BETTING INTERVAL Player 5 now has to accept the inevitable and fold, while players 1 and 2 remain.

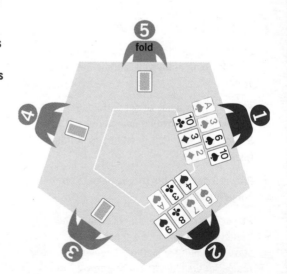

5TH BETTING INTERVAL Player 2 takes the whole pot high-low, but just one card falling differently would have given the pot to player 1.

strategy

Restraint is one of the best virtues you can have in Seven-card Stud, High-low. Weak players will generally stay in far too long, chasing possible high hands and low hands simultaneously, always expecting the card or two they need for a great hand, mostly against all the odds.

It is a good policy to go from the outset for whatever your initial cards suggest – high or low, and if the hand goes wrong, fold. A high hand might develop into a high-low hand, as the specimen deal above showed with player 2's hand. But it is fatal to keep putting in chips just because your hand looks a possibility for both.

So far as the betting goes, don't bet hard if you need specific cards to make your hand, but bet hard when it looks as if your opponent needs specific cards to fill in a gap or two in his hand.

Stud Poker, Lowball

Both Five- and Seven-card Stud (or indeed Stud with any number of cards) can be played as Lowball. The rank of the hands is as for Draw Poker, Lowball (see page 75), i.e. flushes and straights are ignored, so the lowest possible hand is 5, 4, 3, 2, A.

The procedure in both cases is as in regular Stud Poker, with the lowest hand betting first on each round as opposed to the highest.

Because there are fewer ranks of hands, these games are less interesting than the regular or High-low versions.

The strategy in Lowball is to get out with a pair or with a high card. The left-hand illustration on page 108 shows a sample deal at Five-card Stud Lowball. The shaded cards are the hole-cards, known only to their holders, of course.

EXAMPLE
STUD POKER, LOWBALL,
BASIC HAND

first betting interval

1 Player 1 is dealer, so player 4 speaks first
(two 4s are showing as lowest, and player 4 is
the holder of the one nearest to the dealer's
left). He bets.

2 Players 5, 2 and 3 call.

3 Player 1 is not a player to stay in with a King
and folds.

second betting interval

1 Player 3 speaks first (5, A is the lowest hand
showing) and bets.

2 The others call. Player 3's possible flush and
player 5's possible straight are immaterial, as
these don't count in Lowball.

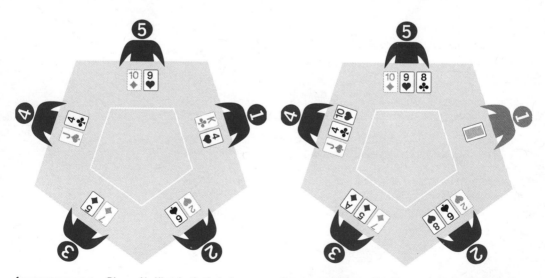

1ST BETTING INTERVAL   Player 1's King in the hole is a
bad card for Lowball, so he will fold.

2ND BETTING INTERVAL   At this stage player 3 has a good
set of low cards, narrowly better than player 2's.

third betting interval

1   Player 3 is still the first to speak, and he bets the maximum. He knows he beats all other hands going into the last round.

2   Player 4 has picked up a pair, and folds.

3   Player 5 knows his hand currently beats that of player 2, and calls.

4   Player 2 folds. He knows that to win he needs both players 3 and 5 (unless they're bluffing) either to get a pair with their last card or to get King or Queen.

fourth betting interval

Player 3 unluckily draws a second Ace. Player 5 has the best hand showing, and is asked to speak first at the last betting interval. He knows that player 3 cannot beat him, and player 3 knows he has lost unless player 5's hole-card is a Queen. It isn't and player 5 takes the pot. A single card can ruin hands in Five-card Stud Lowball.

Of course a single card does not have such a big effect in Seven-card Stud Lowball because of the extra two cards.

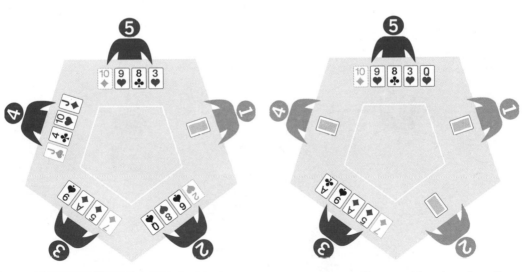

3RD BETTING INTERVAL   Player 3 continues well with a 9, while player 5's 3 helps his hand.

4TH BETTING INTERVAL   The second Ace gives player 3 a pair, and ruins his hand.

English Seven-card Stud

After each player has received two cards face down and three face up, betting after each face-up card, each active player may reject one of his cards and receive another. If he rejects a face-up card his new card is dealt face up, if he rejects a face-down card, his new card is face down, maintaining the two-down, three-up pattern. After a further betting interval each player may reject and receive another card either face up or face down as before. The final betting interval ensues. Players may stand pat, and need not reject a card on the last two rounds, but any player who stands pat on the sixth round must also do so on the seventh.

Mexican Stud or Flip

The first two cards are dealt face down, and each player selects one to turn over as an up card, keeping the second as a hole-card. Everyone does this simultaneously, so one player's choice does not affect anyone else's.

In following rounds (there are commonly five or seven per game) the cards are dealt face down. Each player looks at his new card, and must either turn it face up or switch it with his hole-card, turning his previous hole-card face up. Again, players turn up their chosen cards simultaneously. Betting takes place after each round from the second deal onwards.

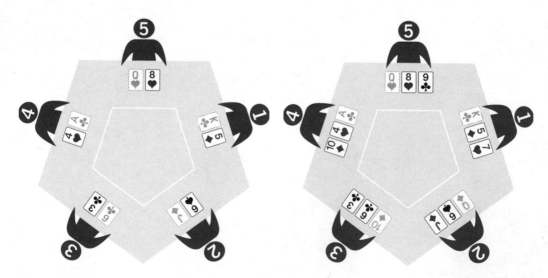

FIRST DEAL Players generally turn over their lower card as an up-card.

SUBSEQUENT DEALS Players choose whether to turn their old hole-card or the new card face up.

minor variations

The number of cards dealt and which of them are face down or face up, and in which order the face-up and face-down cards come, allow other variations in Stud Poker.

The first betting interval always comes after the first up-card, and further betting intervals follow each subsequent card. In all cases players choose five cards from those dealt to them to form their best poker hand.

Five-card Stud

As a variant to the game described above, Five-card Stud is sometimes played with the final card dealt face down, the sequence thus being one down, three up, one down.

Six-card Stud

The sequence of the cards dealt is one down, four up, one down.

Eight-card Stud

The commonest sequence is two down, four up, two down, although it is sometimes two down, four up, one down, one up.

Nine- or Ten-card Stud

Rarely played. The sequence for both is two down, four up and the rest down, although by preference the last card in each case can be dealt face up.

wild cards in Stud

Wild cards may be used in Stud Poker as in other kinds of poker, but the action hardly needs much pepping up, and it is not common.

other forms
of poker

TEXAS HOLD 'EM

Texas Hold 'Em, sometimes called just 'Hold 'Em', has become possibly the best-known form of poker. This is because it is the game played in the World Series of Poker in Binion's Horseshoe Casino in Las Vegas, which has been televised in the United States since the 1980s, and it is also the game played in regular series on two television channels in the United Kingdom. In theory up to 22 people can play but in practice it is rarely played with more than eight.

outline of the game

Each player's object is to make the best poker hand from the two cards he holds and the five common cards in the centre of the table. A player can use both of his hole-cards or one, or if he likes none, using the five common cards as his hand. In this case he is said to be 'playing the board'. He cannot win with this, since the same option is open to all the other players.

In the televised game and in most casinos, a dealer is provided so that none of the players needs to deal. A disc or 'button' is moved round the table deal by deal to indicate who is the nominal dealer. In effect the professional dealer is merely acting for each player in turn. It is customary in casinos, after the cards have been shuffled and cut, for the top card to be 'burned', i.e. discarded unseen. This is to prevent possible cheating.

blind bets

There is no conventional ante, but before any cards are dealt the first two players to the left of the dealer put in small bets known as 'blinds', which is short for blind bets. The first blind, known as the 'small blind', is a percentage of the minimum bet, usually a half or a third, and the second blind, the 'big blind', is usually the table minimum.

When the blinds have been posted (pushed towards the pot) the dealer deals two cards face down to each player. The players examine their cards.

1   The first player to speak in the first betting interval is the one to the left of big blind. He cannot check because a blind bet has been made. He must call, raise or fold. Once the betting has gone all round the table, the two blinds may also call, raise or fold. Small blind must obviously

increase his stake to the level of the betting in order to call. Big blind will have to increase his stake, too, if there has been a raise before the turn reached him.

2 When all bets are equalized, dealer again burns the top card of the pack, and then deals three cards face up to the table. These three are known as the 'flop'. These cards (and the two more, which follow) are common to all players, and are called 'community cards'.

3 A second betting interval now takes place, and in this and subsequent betting intervals, the first player to speak is the nearest active player to the dealer's left, not the first to bet on the previous round, as in Draw Poker.

4 After the second betting interval, and the top card again being burned, a further face-up card is then turned up. This is called the 'turn' or the 'fourth street'. There is another betting interval, another burned card, and a fifth face-up card called 'the river' or 'fifth street'.

5 The final betting interval now takes place, and there is a showdown.

minimum and maximum bets

In a casino, and advisedly in games played socially at home, there will be minimum and maximum bets. In a casino, for example, the small blind might be one chip, the big blind three chips and each bet and raise for that round would be in increments of three chips. Once face-up cards are dealt the bets and raises would be limited to increments of six chips up to the casino limit. The televised games are no-limit knock-out affairs in which all players start with an equal number of chips and continue to play until one player has won all the chips.

For home games the blinds of one chip and three chips are recommended. Since the blinds are regarded as bets it will be necessary for all players to stake at least three chips to stay in for the first round. Three chips could therefore be the minimum bet or raise throughout, with say 10 as the maximum on the first round and 20 once cards are displayed on the table. That gives some scope for bluffing, although not as much as in the no-limit games. The game is also played as a pot-limit game, where the limit for bets and raises is the size of the pot.

jargon-buster

flop the first three of the five community cards, dealt face up in Hold 'Em and Omaha (see page 128).

turn or fourth street the fourth community card in Hold 'Em and Omaha.

river or fifth street the fifth and final community card in Hold 'Em and Omaha.

on the button the notional dealer. In a casino, where a dealer will deal the cards for all players, a disc (known as the button) is passed round the table at each deal to indicate the nominal dealer, who is said to be 'on the button'.

under the gun the first to speak in Hold 'Em and Omaha, where – except in the first betting interval, where he is small blind – the first to speak is always the player to dealer's left, who is said to be 'under the gun'.

small blind the player to dealer's left, who before the deal makes a blind bet of an agreed amount. It also refers to the bet itself.

big blind the player to small blind's left, who before the deal also makes a blind bet of an agreed amount, usually two or three times the amount of the small blind. It also refers to the bet itself.

nut hand or nuts in games where cards are exposed, e.g. Hold 'Em and Omaha, the best hand possible, taking into account a player's hole-cards. For example, if the player held ♥A, ♥2 and the flop showed ♥10, ♥4, ♥3, he would hold the nut flush, an Ace flush being the best possible flush available to any player. He would be holding the nut hand, this being the best hand possible at that stage.

suited if the two cards dealt face down to the player are of the same suit, they are said to be suited.

EXAMPLE
TEXAS HOLD 'EM
BASIC HAND

The stake limits are:

- small blind – one chip
- big blind – three chips
- minimum bet or raise – three chips
- maximum first round bet or raise – ten chips
- maximum bet or raise in other rounds
  – 20 chips

first betting interval

Player 1 is 'on the button', player 2 is small blind and player 3 big blind.

1 **Player 4 is first to speak. He has a very poor hand and folds immediately.**

2 **Player 5 has a reasonably good hand, 10, 9 suited (i.e. of the same suit), and calls.**

3 **Player 1's small pair is also reasonable. He calls.**

4 **Player 2, with A, Q suited, has an excellent hand. Having put in one chip as small blind, he adds two to call, and another three to raise.**

5 **Players 3 and 5 decide to call, as does player 1. Four players are left and there are 24 chips in the pot.**

second betting interval

The flop is a splendid turn-up for player 3, who has a trip (three of a kind) of Jacks.

1 **Player 2 is under the gun, so he speaks first. His hand is now two pairs – Queens and Jacks – but his hopes of a flush have gone. It is not such a good combination as it sounds, since every hand will contain the pair of Jacks, but his two Queens and spare Ace are valuable and he bets three chips, waiting to see how the**

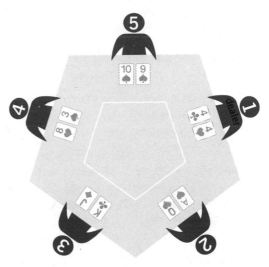

1ST BETTING INTERVAL Player 2's excellent hand leads him to bet positively straight away.

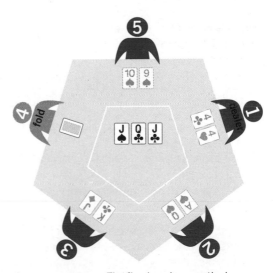

2ND BETTING INTERVAL The flop has done particular favours for players 3 and 5.

betting proceeds. He could have checked, which is an option for all players on all rounds after the first, until somebody bets, when the option disappears.

2 Player 3 has improved to three Jacks, and has King, Queen, Jack of clubs as well. He could hardly have a better hand at this stage but decides that merely to call might pay dividends, if other players remain in.

3 Player 5 has a double-ended straight (Q, J, 10, 9) and three consecutive spades, so he too is happy to stay for three chips.

4 Dealer (player 1), although he has two pairs, Jacks and 4s, is doubtful. He guesses that there must be a hand or two with two pairs around, and he can hardly have the best, since all players have two Jacks, and his two 4s are no good as a second pair. However, he is an optimistic soul, and also calls. Four players are still in and the pot now has 36 chips.

Now comes the turn, or fourth street. It is the ♣10.

third betting interval

Strangely enough, the ♣10, which makes the community cards look exceptional, is not wildly welcomed by most of the players.

1 It does not improve player 2's hand. He checks.

2 Player 3 is happiest. It gives him K, Q, J, 10 suited, with the possibility of the best poker hand of all, a royal flush. He still has no better than his triple Jacks, but a royal flush would be a hand of a lifetime for him. He decides to put some pressure on by betting 20 chips.

3 Player 5's hand is improved to two pairs – Jacks and 10s. He thinks this is not enough, but on the other hand is reluctant to fold, with a Queen-high straight also possible. Without much confidence he calls with 20 chips.

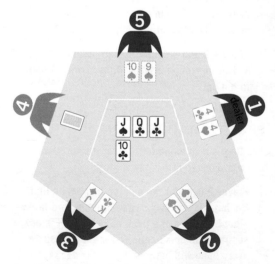

3RD BETTING INTERVAL On the face of it a good card, the turn greatly improves only player 3's hand.

4   The dealer is in a quandary. His two pairs are no good he reckons but a club would give him a flush. On the other hand it might also give another player a flush and if it did so his ♣4 would again be the card that decided the outcome. Sensibly he folds.

5   Player 2, who had checked, now decides to stay in by calling with 20 chips. There are three players in for the final round and a pot of 96 chips.

fourth betting interval

The illustration below shows the community cards when the last card, the fifth street or river, the ♦9, was turned. The whole set of five cards is known as the 'board'.

When the board is displayed, players should work out which two cards could be added to it to make the best hand possible. That hand is known as 'the nuts', and a player who holds it is unbeatable. The best possible hand in this example is a royal flush, needing the ♣A, ♣K in the hole. Nobody has both of these cards. When a pair is showing on the board, a full house is always a good possibility – in this case Queens up would be the best. A flush is likely – it needs only two clubs in the hole. A straight is very likely – a King or 8 in the hole would provide it.

1   Player 2 has been a little unlucky. Two pairs, Queens and Jacks, is less than he would have hoped for with those hole-cards. In view of what hands are possible, he checks.

2   Player 3 has got his straight, but is that enough? He checks, too.

3   Player 5 reckons he has no chance with his two pairs, Jacks and 10s, after the heavy betting. It costs him nothing to check, so the three hands compete in a showdown.

Player 3's straight takes the pot of 96 chips. As he contributed 29 himself, his profit is 67 chips.

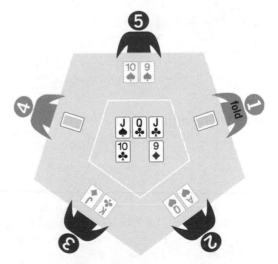

4TH BETTING INTERVAL Player 3's straight outranks the other players' sets of two pairs and he takes the pot.

strategy

In Hold 'Em the first two cards, the face-down ones, are the important ones. All the cards in the board are available to all the players; what separates one player's final hand from another's are the two hole-cards. So the first decision you need to make is the most important.

hole-cards

Since the possible combinations of cards that can be held with two cards is very limited, experts have studied and ranked them, and in 1976 David Sklansky in his book, *Hold 'Em Poker*, graded certain combinations. His ideas have been valued by poker players ever since.

Clearly the best combination to hold in the hole is Ace, Ace. The odds are 220 to 1 against getting this combination, so on average every 220 deals you will hold a hand on which you want to have all the money you can.

After Ace, Ace, the next best hands to hold are a high pair (e.g. K, K or Q, Q) or Ace with a high kicker (e.g. A, K, or A, Q).

pairs

Pairs are valuable, as there is always the possibility of improving to a triple on the flop. Pairs come round on average every 17 hands and if you stay in you can expect your pair to become a trip on the flop once in 8.8 times (odds of nearly 8 to 1 against).

When it comes to evaluating pairs, there are big gaps in value between Aces and Kings, and between Kings and Queens. After these, Jacks, 10s and 9s can be regarded as medium pairs, 8s and below small ones.

Ace with high kicker

More valuable than medium or small pairs is an Ace with a high kicker, i.e. Ace and King or Ace and Queen, particularly if they are suited. For example, if you have Ace, King and an Ace or King appears in the flop, you hold the top pair, because if the pair is Aces, your King is the highest kicker, and if the pair is Kings, then your Ace is the highest kicker. Only a triple, a flush or a straight can beat you. This is a good hand to bet on. Ace, Queen will be beaten if an Ace flops and an opponent holds Ace, King. Ace with a medium kicker of Jack, 10 or 9 can be useful and would be a good hand to bet on, but an Ace with a bigger kicker will beat you. Once you get down to Ace, Jack or Ace, 10, then you consider that a pair of Jacks or 10s would be a better pair of hole-cards.

Ace with small kicker

An Ace with a small kicker, if they are not suited, is not a particularly good hand, and ranks below a combination with potential for flushes or straights. An Ace with a small kicker suited is, however, much more valuable, because of its potential for an Ace-high flush. For instance, if you hold Ace, 3 suited and three or more of the suit appear in the board you hold the top flush. If instead you held King, 3 you are in danger of losing to an opponent with Ace of the suit among his hole-cards. And according to the other cards on the board, Ace-high flush could be the nuts.

unpaired high cards

Hands such as King, Queen and King, 10 etc. are hands that might be the best-ranking hands before the flop but that can lead to problems, particularly if unsuited. For instance, suppose you hold King, Jack, you could flop a King and have the highest pair, but if you flopped a Jack, unless the other flopped cards are smaller, it is much less likely. Jack, 10, suited, with its potential for a flush and a straight is better to hold, say, a small pair. If you hold a card below a 9 and it is not suited to an Ace, you are in the second class when it comes to rank of hands.

flush and straight

Straights and flushes can win the pot, but when you hold two cards that are suited or consecutive, you have a long way to go to fill a five-card flush or straight. These combinations are sometimes called 'drawing hands' because you need to draw a series of cards to improve them. Obviously, if they are consecutive and suited it is a better bet than if they are one or the other. Combinations from 9, 8 suited down to 5, 4 suited are worth about the same as a small pair. Suited cards that cannot be part of a straight, such as 9, 4 or 10, 2, might be better folded sooner rather than later. When it comes to consecutive cards that are unsuited, then obviously the higher the better, with anything lower than Queen, Jack being valued less than a small pair.

other combinations

If you hold two cards neither of which is high (so Jack and below), and if they are not suited and there are gaps between them (Jack, 4 or 9, 6), then they should not be bet upon. It doesn't follow that all other hands are worth betting. For example 7, 6 unsuited or 3, 2 suited is not worth risking cash.

position

In Hold 'Em, your position at the table relative to the dealer is important. The nearer you are to the dealer's right the better, because there are fewer players to speak after you. The dealer acts last on each round (except the first, when big blind is last to speak), so has the best position of all.

Most hands you get will be middling, but suppose you get something a little better, say Ace, 10, and sitting after big blind you call. A later player raises, another calls and you call. The flop reveals 9, 6, 4, which are of no help to you. You check and the other two players bet. Your best option now is to fold. One opponent has possibly paired, another is sitting with Ace, King, say, and all you have is Ace, 10. However, if you were last to speak against two opponents and they check, your Ace, 10 now looks much better. A bet might force them to fold. To bet in the early positions therefore requires a better hand than in the later positions.

strategy before the flop

If you are a tight player, you might decide that you will enter the betting only with a pair, two cards both 10 or higher or a suited Ace. A looser player might bet with two smaller cards if they are consecutive cards that are suited, as ♣8, ♣7. Remember you need a better hand when first to speak then you do if last, because in subsequent rounds you will be betting before strong opponents and likely to be facing difficult decisions.

strategy after the flop

The flop is where the hand is made or broken. A good pair of hole-cards can become worthless, a moderate hand can become very strong.

if the flop hasn't helped

The first advice is to fold if the flop hasn't helped, leaving you holding nothing. Forget what a good hand you held before the flop – that is over.

if the flop helps a little

Suppose the flop leaves you with a medium pair and outside chances of a straight or flush by picking up the right card or cards on fourth and fifth streets. Again the policy would be to fold.

For example, you hold ♣9, ♣8. The flop is ♥9, ♦A, ♣J. You now have a pair of 9s, a possible flush (two clubs required), a possible straight (10 with Queen or 7 required), a possible triple of 9s etc. But if others are betting there is likely to be a pair of Aces or Jacks around already beating you. And if fourth street brings you a Queen and the next round brings a bet and raise will you want to put in chips in the hope of a 10 on fifth street?

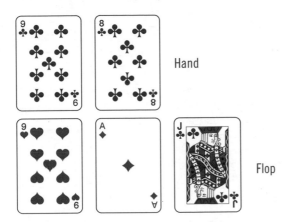

Hand

Flop

On the whole, hoping to fill straights or flushes, or holding on to a pair when there is a higher card in the flop, are poor bets and especially so when there is no limit or pot limit. You do not want to be in a position of having to call a huge bet with cards like that.

It is also as well to remember that all the communal cards are just that – they belong to you all. If a pair of Aces appears in the flop, remember everybody's hand is a pair of Aces high, and possibly somebody holds two pairs already. If you are holding ♥J, ♥10, and the flop is ♣A, ♦A, ♣4, you are unlikely to be holding the best hand.

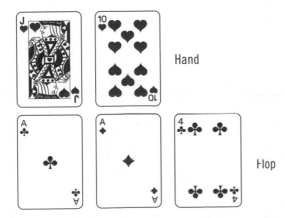

Hand

Flop

if the flop does help you

The other side of all these warnings, of course, is that if the flop does help you, then bet. If you've bet on, say, 9, 9, and the flop comes up 9, Q, 2, it is worth betting.

Suppose you hold A, K and there is an Ace in the flop. This is an excellent hand to bet. You have the top pair with the top kicker, so you are in a very strong position. It's going to take a triple, or more likely two pairs, to beat you.

A similar situation pertains when holding a pair and there is no card higher in the flop than the rank of your pair. For example you hold Q, Q and the flop is 9, 6, J. Unless somebody has two Aces or two Kings in the hole, you must have the best pair out. But it's a hand that could trap you into betting too enthusiastically because if an Ace or King appears in the fourth or fifth street, your two Queens are likely not to be the best pair any more.

Similarly, if you have a moderate pair in the hole and are lucky enough to hit a triple in flop, do not think that's that. The other two flop cards could prove vital. Suppose you hold 9, 9. The flop comes up A, Q, 9. There is a chance that the Ace and/or Queen have provided someone with a higher triple or, more likely, that they are at least paired, with the chance of another on fourth or fifth street to beat your triple. On the other hand you are in a much better position if the flop is 8, 9, 2, especially if these are of differing suits. Now your hand is certainly best at the moment. It is worth betting here. You will be hoping an opponent with, say, A, 8 will raise you. A bigger triple than 9 is unlikely, and a flush is unlikely, as nobody can be holding four of a suit yet. You will win far more than you lose.

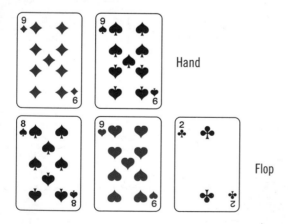

Hand

Flop

Suppose your hand and the flop provide you with two pairs in this manner: you hold 4, 4 and the flop comes up K, 7, 7. Two pairs looks good, but do not forget that everybody has one pair: the 7s. If one player has a King in the hole, your only chance to win is with a full house or four of a kind. You need the turn or the river to be a 4. In effect, the flop has not improved your hand much.

But suppose your two pairs came like this: your hole-cards are ♦10, ♦9. The flop is ♣9, ♥K, ♠10. Things are looking better. You probably hold the best hand now. But there are dangers ahead. An opponent may hold K, 10 or K, 9 which will almost certainly mean you are going to lose. And a holding of Q, J would give an opponent a straight. Even an opponent with one or other of Q, J has two chances to fill a straight. You could raise with this hand, however, and hope to scare off everybody but the opponent who holds, say, K, 6 and is betting on his pair of Kings. Even then a 6 at the turn or river would need you to complete a full house to win.

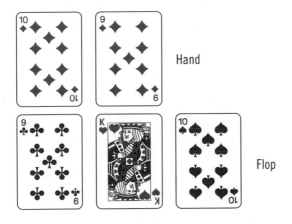

Hand

Flop

fourth street

There is often little action once you get to fourth street, as quite frequently the hands that are still in are not improved. You have to watch out for possible flushes. If the flop contains two cards of the same suit and the turn provides a third, there is a possibility that an opponent might hold a flush. You must beware. If he checks, he might have a flush and be bluffing to lead you to bet. It would be best to check. If he bets, you still must make the decision as to whether he holds a flush or is bluffing. So it is now down to how well you know each other as to how you act. Of course, he too will wonder if you hold a flush. Do you try to bluff him?

fifth street

The same applies to fifth street as fourth street. You either have the hand now or you don't. The chance of a player finding himself with a flush or a straight by the back door, i.e. by completing the hand by accident with favourable cards on the turn and river, is always a possibility. Suddenly and unexpectedly a hand is transformed and betting comes alive again.

Even expert players can sometimes be caught out by these back-door miracles. On one of the big knock-out televised events an expert, who was 'all-in' (i.e. all his chips were in the pot), stood up and shook hands with his opponent, thinking he was eliminated, not having realized that the river had completed a winning straight for him. Of course, he played on. It was the cards that counted – not the blip of his having misread them.

bluffing

Anyone who has watched televised Hold 'Em Poker games will have seen bluffing come into its own. Some of the bigger pots have been won by the worst hand. This is because of the no-limit format of the game.

Blinds are used and, as the game advances, the amounts required for them increase. The player with the fewest chips is likely to find that he has to force himself into the action, because if he goes more than a round or two without betting his pile will get eaten up in blinds. Occasionally he is forced into a bluff. Equally, once a player's pile looks vulnerable, players with more chips try to bluff him out of hands, knowing that he will be reluctant to stake his diminishing stack of chips on inferior hands.

jargon-buster

bicycle or wheel the best low hand in Hold 'Em and Omaha High-low games; any 5, 4, 3, 2, A, the suits being immaterial.

case the fourth card of a rank in games like Stud and Hold 'Em where there are face-up cards. If, for example, there are three 9s showing on the table, or two 9s are exposed and a player holds a third as a hole-card, the fourth 9 is referred to as the 'case 9'.

back door a player who, usually inadvertently, completes a flush or a straight with the last two community cards in Hold 'Em and Omaha, is said to have done so 'by the back door'.

EXAMPLE
BIG BLUFF

Player 2 has contributed 4,000 chips to the pot as small blind and player 3 8,000 chips as big blind.

first betting interval

1 **Player 4 folds.**

2 **Player 5 raises 10,000 chips.**

3 **Player 1 (dealer) folds, as does player 2.**

4 **Player 3, whose pile is getting somewhat low, decides this is the optimum time to bluff. He calls. There are now 40,000 chips in the pot.**

The flop comes ♣A, ♦9, ♠2.

second betting interval

1 **Player 3 goes 'all-in', with 45,000 chips. The pot is now 85,000 chips and if player 5 calls, that will be the end of the betting. The players would expose their cards, the dealer would expose fourth and fifth street together, and the better hand would take the pot. If player 5 wins, player 3 is out of the competition.**

2 **So what does player 5 do? We know both hands so it is obvious to us he should call the bet, as he is favourite. But the fact that player 3 called his original raise and then went all-in after the flop suggests to player 5 that he has probably paired an Ace, which would make player 5's chances very small indeed. In fact, he needs fourth and fifth streets to help him: Q, 10 or 10, 8 for a straight or K, J for two pairs, which might not win anyway. Is it worth risking 45,000 chips in case player 3 is bluffing?**

The chances are that player 5 will fold, and player 3 will pick up the pot of 85,000 on a hand of ♠6, ♣3. Of course, only 22,000 of that is winnings, but he has retrieved his big blind and is fine for another round or two.

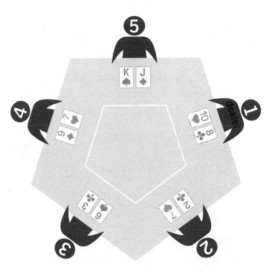

1ST BETTING INTERVAL   Player 3 has the worst hand at the moment and has an almost negligible chance of winning the hand.

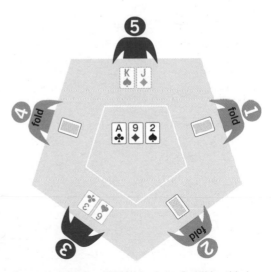

2ND BETTING INTERVAL   With only player 5 still in, this is an ideal time for player 3 to bluff.

OMAHA

Omaha is a game of increasing popularity, possibly approaching Seven-card Stud and Texas Hold 'Em as being one of the most widely played versions of Poker. It is a new phenomenon, and many authoritative textbooks published before the 1980s fail to mention it. The higher number of cards from which the final Poker hand can be made, and therefore the chance of holding better hands, are the reasons for its success.

outline of the game

Omaha is a very similar game to Texas Hold 'Em – the difference lies in the number of hole-cards and so the number of cards available for making the final hand.

1 After the usual preliminaries of shuffle, cut and the top card being burned, four cards are dealt face down to each player. One of the anteing systems is used (i.e. either all put in, dealer puts in, or there's a small and big blind, etc.). Players examine their hole-cards and a betting interval takes place.

2 Three community cards (the flop) are then dealt face up to the table. There is then a second betting interval.

3 A fourth community card (the turn) is then dealt face up to the table and a third betting interval takes place.

4 A fifth and final community card (the river) is then dealt face up to the table and a fourth and final betting interval takes place.

5 There is then a showdown, and the player with the best five-card poker hand wins.

So the game is identical to Texas Hold 'Em except that each player has nine cards (four hole-cards and five community cards) instead of seven from which to make his best hand. However, there is a restriction: players must use two of their hole-cards and three of the community cards.

This seemingly small difference from Texas Hold 'Em does, in fact, make Omaha a more complex game and new players should familiarize themselves with the possible hands before playing for money.

sample hand 1

The player with the hand below finds his hole-cards offer the promise of the top flush in hearts – he needs three hearts from the five community cards to come. After the flop, he still has this possibility, but also now has the chance of various straights, requiring a 9 or 6. The turn destroys his chance of a heart flush, but completes a straight. However, the river gives him a fifth spade, making his best hand a back-door Queen flush.

Flushes and straights are common in Omaha, since if three cards of a suit, for example, appear in the five communal cards, it only requires one player to hold two more of that suit among his four hole-cards to have a flush.

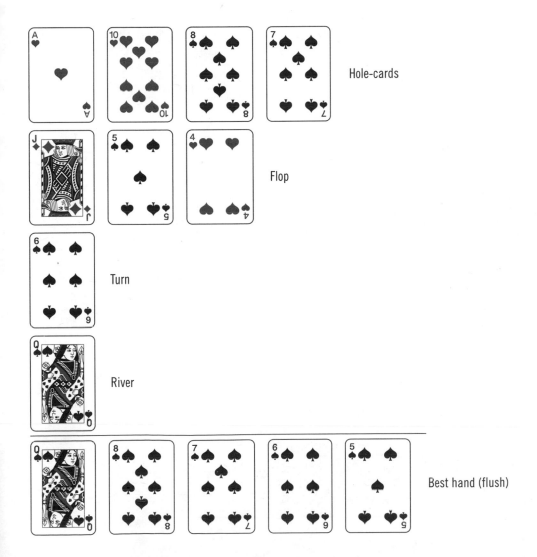

Hole-cards

Flop

Turn

River

Best hand (flush)

sample hand 2

The hand below contains three 10s and an Ace, but the holder cannot think of the chance of four of a kind, or even a full house, because he cannot use all three 10s. Remember, he can use only two of his hole-cards. In effect he would be better off holding a pair of 10s rather than three. The flop comes up with another Ace, but, of course, this doesn't give him a full house. Two pairs, even Aces up, would not win many deals of Omaha. Still available is an Ace flush in hearts. The turn is useless, but the river provides another Ace.

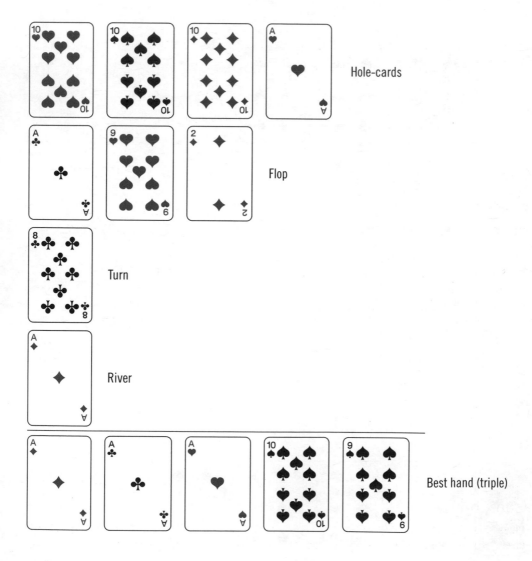

Hole-cards

Flop

Turn

River

Best hand (triple)

This unlucky player now holds three Aces and three 10s, but still cannot claim a full house. He must use exactly two hole-cards, so can claim the triple Aces but can use only one of the 10s. His best hand is as shown. Although the communal cards show that there is no chance of a player holding a flush (there aren't three cards suited), and no chance of a straight (there aren't three cards that could be used to form one), the triple Aces are not sure to win. Every player will have the two Aces at his disposal. A player who holds the fourth Ace and a card higher than 10 will beat the hand, as will a player who holds the fourth Ace with 9, 8, or 2, as well as one who holds a pair of 9s, 8s or 2s, because he will complete a full house.

EXAMPLE
BASIC OMAHA GAME

Bets and raises are one to three chips for the first two intervals and three to ten chips for intervals three and four. Player 1 is dealer, and there is an ante of five chips.

first betting interval

Player 2 speaks first, and bets two chips. All players call. There are 15 chips in the pot.

flop

The flop comes up ♦9, ♠3 and ♥J.

second betting interval

1 **Player 2, if all cards could count, would have a straight, but must 'discard' two of his**

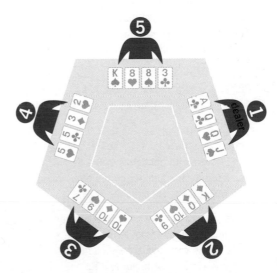

1ST BETTING INTERVAL At this stage all the players are content to remain in the game.

hole-cards. He nevertheless can fill a straight with any 8 or 10 and has other possible straights, including a straight flush. Player 2 bets two chips.

2   Player 3's hand has not improved much, as the 9 in his hole will probably not help him, but he has four chances of a straight, especially with an 8. Therefore he calls.

3   Player 4 folds. He is not helped by the flop.

4   Player 5 is not helped, but also calls. He has his two 8s, and three spades towards a flush.

5   Player 1 still has his pair of Queens, and Queen is the highest card he can see, so he also calls.

Four players are left in and the pot is 23 chips.

the turn

Next comes the turn, the ♠9. This changes the nature of some hands.

third betting interval

1   Player 2 now has triple 9s. He has a good chance of a full house on the river, needing a K, Q or 10, and he still has chances of a straight. He decides to bet the limit of ten chips.

2   Player 3 is in a similar situation, having three 9s and wanting a 10 or 7 for a full house. He calls.

3   Player 5 has two pairs, 9s and 8s and can fill a full house with another 9 or 8 – he also has four spades, and another on the river would give him a flush. He calls.

4   Player 1 also has two pairs, Queens and 9s, and decides to call, too. He reckons if either turns up, he will have a good chance of winning. He calls. The pot is 63 chips.

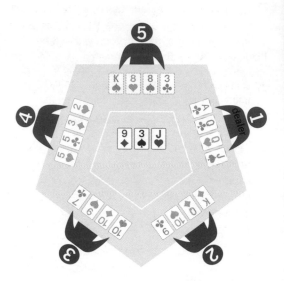

2ND BETTING INTERVAL   The flop has not actually helped any of the players much.

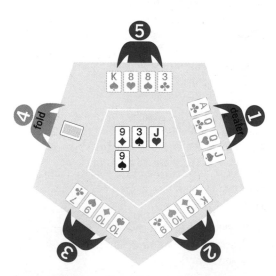

3RD BETTING INTERVAL   The ♠9 has improved most players' hands, but they need to bear in mind that everyone now has at least a pair of 9s.

- Players 1 and 5 are being a trifle optimistic with their two pairs, because if a 9 appears on the river, all players will hold three 9s, with the possibility that an opponent is holding four. Player 5, however, still has the chance of a winning flush.

- Player 2 has most options of significant improvement with the outstanding 9 (called the 'case 9') providing four of a kind, any of three remaining three Kings, three Queens and three 10s providing a full house and any of three 8s providing a straight. Thirteen of the unknown cards will improve his hand. (Remember all players can see only eight cards, their hole-cards and the four communal cards turned so far.)

- Player 5 needs a 9 for a full house, or any of nine spades for a flush, so has ten chances to improve his hand.

- Player 3 can get the case 9 for a set of four, or one of two 10s or three 7s for a full house, making 6 chances to improve his hand.

- Player 1 can get the case 9 for a full house or one of two Queens for a full house, Queens up; only three chances to improve his hand significantly. Improving to a better two pairs has not been considered.

With sight of all four hands, plus the discarded hand, we can see that there is no chance of four 9s, as all four 9s are accounted for.

We can work out all players' chances, bearing in mind that player 2 has the best hand at the moment, triple 9s, K, J.

- Player 1 can beat this with ♠Q (full house, Queens, 9s) or ♦J, or ♣J (triple Jacks) – 3 chances in 28.

- Player 3 can beat this with ♣10 (full house, 10s, 9s) or ♠7, ♦7, or ♥7 (full house, 9s, 7s). He has 4 chances in 28.

- Player 5 can beat this with ♠A, ♠6, ♠5, ♠4 or ♠2 for a flush (not ♠Q, which wins for player 1 or ♠7, which wins for player 3) or ♦8, ♣8, (full house 8s, 9s). Note he does not win with ♥3, because to get a full house of 3s, 8s, he would need to use three of his hole-cards. He has 7 chances in 28.

- All other cards (14) win for player 2, whether he improves his hand or not.

Thus player 2 has exactly an even chance of taking the pot, player 5 is 21 to 7, or 3 to 1 against, player 3 is 24 to 4, or 6 to 1 against, and player 1 is 25 to 3, or more than 8 to 1 against.

If all of them knew these odds (and they don't because, unlike us, they cannot see the other players' cards), player 2 would bet the maximum of ten chips again. Player 3, seeing he would need to put in ten chips to win a pot of 73 would call, as his chances are only 6 to 1 against. Player 5, with a pot now of 83, is offered odds of 8 to 1 for a 3 to 1 chance and would call, or even raise, and player 1, with a pot now of at least 93 chips could just about justify calling, too.

Thus the pot would stand at 103 chips or more when the river is turned over. Who wins? Justice would say player 2, but luck also plays a part in poker.

strategy

Much of the skill in Omaha comes in recognizing what constitutes a good hand. Unlike Texas Hold 'Em, in which efforts have been made to grade the two-card hands held before the flop, the rules of Omaha make the four-card hands – of which two cards only, no more, no fewer, may be used – impossible to evaluate precisely. One can only know what a good hand, as opposed to a poor one, is.

A good hand consists of four cards that work with each other, giving opportunities to develop hands with the flop in many directions.

For example, see the hand below. With this, depending on the flop, you have a range of chances:

- triple or four Aces.

- two cards to six straights from different flops: Q, 9, 8 – 9, 8, 7 – K, Q, J – A, K, Q – K, Q, 10 – K, Q, 9.

- two cards to Ace flushes – in fact these will be nut flushes because there cannot be two flushes of different suits in Omaha, since a flush requires three suited cards among the community cards, and there cannot be sets of three suited cards among five cards in two different sets.

 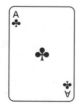 

betting hard

A good hand in Omaha requires aggressive betting. Getting opponents to fold and picking up pots is generally a better policy than checking in the hope of persuading others to put in more chips. The more opponents who get more cards the more likely it is that one of them will hit an even better hand than yours.

Obviously the best holding before the flop involves two cards of one suit and two of another, with all four cards connected or paired, with potentials for runs. The hand below is a good example of this. If you have one or two cards unconnected to the others by suit or rank, clearly the hand is not so good. Because you can use only two of your hole-cards in making your hand, two Aces is actually better than three. With three Aces, one cannot be used, and there is only one left in the pack to achieve a triple with the remaining two.

After the flop you must look at your possible trips, full houses, flushes and straights in the same manner. Work out roughly, if not exactly, how many ways you can achieve these hands, without forgetting that communal cards are exactly that. If two Queens among the five common ones give you triple Queens, remember an opponent might well have triple Queens, too. If you have two Aces to go with them, fine. If your best to accompany them is, say, Jack on the board and 7 in hand, beware.

Five- and Six-card Omaha

Five- and Six-card Omaha are played as described above with the exception that instead of four face-down cards each player receives five or six. The possibilities of making good hands are much greater, since each player has ten or 11 cards from which to make his hand (although a hand must still be composed of two hole-cards and three communal cards).

Omaha can also be played as Lowball or High-low. Lowball is played like the parent game, but the lowest hand wins. As in versions of Lowball previously described, flushes and straights are not considered as hands, the lowest hand therefore being 5, 4, 3, 2, A.

Omaha High-low Eight or Better

This is a distinctive and interesting game. At the showdown the highest hand wins half the pot, and the lowest hand wins half the pot. A player has no need to specify whether he is going for high or low, and indeed can try for each with different hands. For example, a player may use any two of his hole-cards and any three from the community cards to form his hand for high and a different set to form his hand for low, provided there are two hole-cards and three community cards in each hand.

The 'eight' in the title refers to the fact that only hands that are 8 high or better can compete for low, i.e. a hand that does not contain five cards of differing ranks all 8 or below is ineligible.

In the two hands below, player 2 wins the high with his triple 4s (he cannot use his ♠A with the ♣A to make a full house, as he would be using three hole-cards). Player 1 can do no better than a pair of Aces. However, player 1 wins the low with 7, 5, 4, 2, A (the Ace he has to use is ♣A, as he cannot use 7, 2, from his hole-cards and ♥A, as well). Player 2 is ineligible for low, as he can get no lower than Queen high. If no players in the showdown can compete for low, the winner of high takes the whole pot.

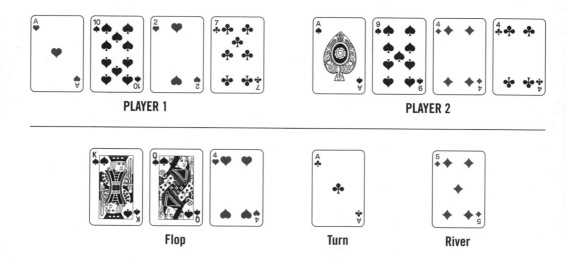

PLAYER 1   **PLAYER 2**

Flop   **Turn**   **River**

EXAMPLE
OMAHA HIGH-LOW EIGHT
OR BETTER BASIC HAND

Player 1 is dealer, and player 2 puts in one chip as small blind and player 3 two chips as big blind.

Bets and raises are two chips before and after the flop, but there is a maximum of five chips after the turn. There is also a limit of three raises per player during one betting interval.

first betting interval

Player 4 speaks first and calls, and all other players call. The pot is 10 chips.

The flop appears.

second betting interval

1 Player 2 speaks first, and has paired Queens and 5s. He bets two chips.

2 Player 3's hand looks good, as he needs only an Ace, 3 or 4 to complete the best low hand, and a heart to complete an Ace flush. He calls and raises two.

3 Player 4 is in the same position regarding low, and calls.

4 Player 5 folds.

5 Player 1 sees opportunities for straights and has paired his Queen, so he optimistically calls, too.

6 Player 2 calls. The pot is now 26 chips.

The turn is an Ace.

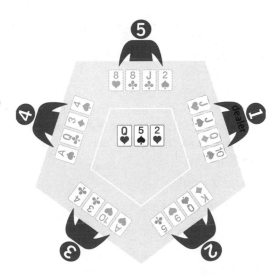

AFTER THE FLOP   Player 5's hand is the only one that has little chance either high or low.

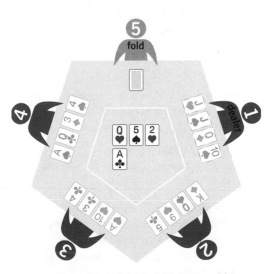

THE TURN   The ♣A is helpful for both high and low hands.

third betting interval

1 **Player 2 is not helped, but bets two chips.**

2 **Player 3 has now completed his low, the best possible, a bicycle, and raises five chips.**

3 **Player 4 has done the same. He also raises five chips.**

4 **Player 1 folds – he still holds only a pair of Queens. Although he thinks players are betting on low, it is a reasonable bet that one of them will have a pair of Aces and be beating him for high, too.**

5 **Player 2 calls.**

6 **Player 3 calls and raises another five chips.**

7 **Player 4 raises another five.**

8 **Player 2 is in a fix. He knows players 3 and 4 are betting on low, and his two pairs are likely good for high, although either opponent might also hold two pairs, Aces up. He realizes the odds are against him and folds.**

9 **Player 3 makes his final raise.**

10 **Player 4 does the same.**

11 **Player 3's final call ends the betting. The pot is now 102 chips.**

fourth betting interval

The river is turned to the horror of player 2. Had he stayed in he would have completed a full house and be practically certain to win high.

1 **The card is significant for player 3, too, as it completes a nut flush for him. He bets five chips.**

2 **Player 4 merely calls. He realizes the chances are that the low pot will be shared, and his high hand is no better than his low hand. He notices that his opponent might hold a flush. The pot ends at 112 chips.**

THE RIVER The ♥5 has worked out perfectly for player 3 who wins high and shares low with player 4.

So player 3 takes 56 chips for high, as his best hand, ♥A, ♥Q, ♥10, ♥5, ♥2, an Ace flush, beats player 4's run of A, 2, 3, 4, 5. This run is also, of course, both player's hand for low, the pot for which they share at 28 chips each. So player 4, with his unbeatable low hand, gets only a quarter of the pot. Player 3 collects 84 chips, a profit of 41, and player 4 collects 28 chips, and loses 15.

poker sense

POKER SENSE

This last section on poker includes some final words on bluffing, which have been mentioned in various places already, and a little on etiquette.

bluffing

Poker is known to be a game of bluff, and newcomers are apt to believe that you cannot win without bluffing. If they watch big games on television they will see big bluffs working. It looks easy. When they start to play, they will probably bluff too often, or at least at the wrong times, and will soon begin to wonder why their opponents aren't falling for the sort of ploy that seems to work on TV.

It is true that bluffing and psychology play a bigger role in poker than any other card game. Psychology is the knack of 'reading' your opponents and being able to discern from their demeanour or style of play how strong their hands are. This, of course, is easier with players you've known for a long time, and played with often, than it is with strangers. With the former it is easier for you to detect if an opponent might be bluffing. But this is only part of the game. The best confidence trickster in the world cannot win consistently at poker merely by bluffing. Bluffing is not a winner in itself, but used at the right times and in the right circumstances it can pay rich dividends.

As stated earlier, there are two kinds of bluffing:

1 To fool your opponents that your hand is better than it is.

2 To fool your opponents that your hand is not so good.

In the first example, your purpose is to avoid a showdown. You bet heavily, your opponent thinks he is beaten and folds. Perhaps he had the better hand, but you pick up the pot. You do not need to show your hand, so he never knows if he was bluffed or not.

mind games

However, if you work a successful bluff, perhaps at times you might want your opponent to know it. You are now entering the realm of mind games. Normally he would not know that you had been bluffing, but if you expose your hand, he will see he has been bluffed. He will not like it. You then refrain from bluffing for a while, in the hope that similar circumstances will arise when your hand is a good one. This time you hope your opponent, remembering how he was bluffed before, and not wanting to be bluffed again, will bet with you, and force a showdown. This time you have the cards, and win a bigger pot than you would otherwise.

Remember certain things when thinking of bluffing

NUMBER OF PLAYERS

The more players there are left in the pot, the harder it is to bring off a successful bluff. The reason is clear. If three opponents are left, and you frighten off two, but one remains to take the pot, it is no good reflecting that your bluff was two-thirds successful. You do not get two-thirds of the pot.

POSITION

It is really making the same point to say that position at the table is important.

- If you are 'under the gun', all the other players are still in the game. Running a bluff from here is very difficult.

- On the other hand if you are last to speak and only one player has bet, a maximum raise might well persuade him to fold, leaving you the pot with nothing in your hand.

As an example, suppose you are the last person to speak before the draw in Jackpots Draw Poker, holding a pair of 4s. All but one of your opponents has folded. The man who bet must have a pair of Jacks or better. Suppose you raise and he calls.

1 He takes three cards (suggesting he held a pair).

2 You take one (pretending you held two pairs, or four to a flush or straight).

3 He bets and you raise the maximum. If his best is still just a pair, however high (the odds are 5 to 2 against him having improved), will he be prepared to risk a sizeable number of chips on calling? Or will he assume you've filled a flush, straight or even a full house, or at least still have two pairs, and save his money?

If bluffing to urge opponents to fold, you must be prepared to raise, forcing opponents to spend money to discover whether you are bluffing or not. Calling will not frighten anybody away.

WHEN TO BLUFF

You have seen the opportunity to bluff your opponent, and have forced him to make a decision. Of course, before you tried your bluff, you would have estimated that your opponent was likely to fold. There are some players, not good ones, who are so frightened of losing to a bluff, that they will call in almost any circumstances. Many times they will lose money – but that's no consolation to you if you are bluffing and they win on this occasion. So choose carefully when to bluff. Newcomers to the game are particularly loath to be bluffed, so they will often call you out to your irritation, while an experienced player accepts that he will be bluffed occasionally.

good games for bluffing

It is far easier to bluff in no-limit or pot-limit games than in games with a limit. Suppose the pot contains 100 chips in a limit game, and your bet or raise is limited to, say, five chips. Very few opponents are prepared to be bluffed out of a pot of that size if it costs only five chips to call. To most the five chips would be worth the peace of mind that comes from knowing they were really beaten. To save the five and spend the rest of the week wondering if they were bluffed or not is not an option.

bluffing to lose

Some players advocate the value of bluffing in the expectation of losing, in order to persuade opponents you are a loose player and encourage them to bet against you next time, when your hand is a winner. But this seems unnecessary. You will find that enough bluffs fail when you are trying to win to make it unnecessary for you to 'deliberately' lose a few more. The contrary advice, given by other players, is that you should only stay in the game if you believe your hand is the best one held at the table. But that would preclude this form of bluffing altogether.

The best advice is that all your bets should be aimed at winning the pot. Do not bluff in hope, bluff with purpose.

So you must consider the size of the pot before bluffing. The bigger the pot grows in limit poker the harder it becomes to bluff an opponent out of it. So the best bluffs are those that get rid of opponents early, particularly in Stud Poker, before their hands can develop.

In no-limit knockout games, such as Hold 'Em or Omaha, with progressively larger blind bets, a player whose pile of chips gets low is often obliged to bluff. If he waits for the good hands, he sees his pile diminishing as he is called upon to provide each of the two blinds every round. Since he will get knocked out if he doesn't bet, sooner or later he will choose a time to go 'all-in', i.e. bet all his chips on one hand. Sometimes he cannot wait for a good hand to arrive, and stakes all on a poor one. If he is called by an opponent who senses his predicament, he can only hope the board is kind to him, and turns up cards that convert his poor hand into a winning one. This is one of those situations that make the game so fascinating: everything depends on whether one player is bluffing or not, and whether the other players can tell.

bluffing to look weak

The second type of bluff where you lead your opponents to believe your hand is weaker than it is in order to get more money into the pot, is probably more useful, especially in limit poker, where you need to build up the pot you expect to win. You therefore bet slowly, perhaps call where you might have raised, to encourage opponents to stay in the game longer. An example of slow playing is given overleaf.

If you are sure you have the best hand, the object is to keep your opponents betting.

- If you bet the maximum at every opportunity there is a danger that all your opponents will fold, leaving you with a lower pot than you would like.

- If you bet too low and nobody raises, again you may not have made the best of your hand.

There is no rule you can follow in this situation. Your judgement of the other players and how they are betting is your guide.

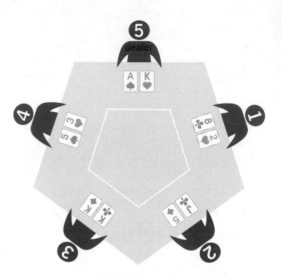

1ST BETTING INTERVAL Two Kings is an excellent start, and player 3 is right to bet positively on them.

EXAMPLE
SLOW PLAYING

The game is Texas Hold 'Em and there is no limit. Player 5 is dealer. Small blind (player 1) puts in five chips and big blind (player 2) puts in 10 chips.

first betting interval

1 Player 3, with his two Kings, bets 20 chips.

2 Player 5 raises 20, and all the others fold.

second betting interval

1 At the flop Player 3 completes triple Kings. He decides on a slow-play bluff and checks.

2 Player 5, with two Kings, an Ace kicker, and the chance of a straight, bets 50 chips.

3 Player 3 calls.

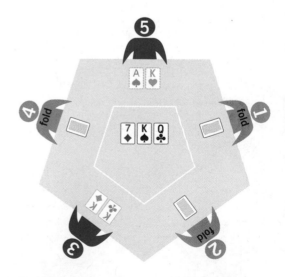

2ND BETTING INTERVAL With such a good hand, player 3 decides to play slow in order to entice player 5 to bet further.

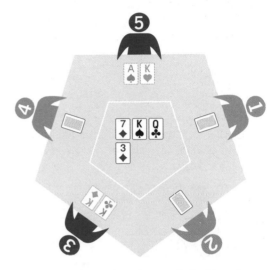

3RD BETTING INTERVAL The 3 does not help either player.

third betting interval

1 **The turn helps neither and both check.**

fourth betting interval

1 **The river, too, is neutral. Player 3 checks again.**

2 **Player 5 bets 100 chips. He has two pairs, Kings up, and reckons player 3, on his tentative betting, can have no better than the same, in which case player 5's Ace kicker will be vital.**

3 **Player 3, having sprung the trap, raises 200 chips and whatever player 5 does now, will win an excellent pot. Had player 3 not checked twice and called once, player 5 probably would not have bet so confidently against him.**

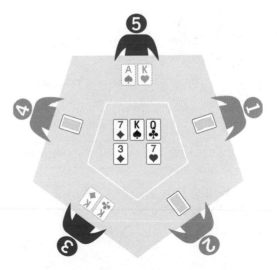

4TH BETTING INTERVAL Player 5 falls for player 3's bluff, thinks his two pairs are unbeatable and bets heavily.

key rules of poker etiquette

Poker is a game where money can change hands in large sums very quickly, leading to strong emotions. In the old Wild West these might have led to six-shooters being drawn. To prevent the modern equivalent of a gunfight, standards of behaviour are expected at the table, and some are noted here.

- At all times play should be seen to be above board.

- Each player is responsible for his own cards and chips (or cash), and should keep both in full view at all times.

- A player should not show his cards to another player who might have folded, or hold them out of sight of others. When not being examined, they should be face down on the table. Nor should chips (or cash) be secreted away in pockets – they should be on the table at all times.

- A player should not touch another player's cards or chips.

- Players should not discard cards, or make any action indicating their intent to do so, out of turn.

- Players should not call or bet out of turn. Any such act might clearly affect the decisions of other players.

- When discarding, a player should make sure that other players have no chance to see which cards he has discarded.

- Ideally at no time should a player show his cards except at a showdown. If, after the showdown, a player who folded and therefore took no part in it, feels the need (often in exasperation) to show the hand he folded then all other players must see it, not just his particular friends.

- A player should not discuss a hand while it is in progress, even if he has folded.

- Making misleading remarks is bad form. Saying something like 'I'll risk a little on an Ace' when holding three kings, is regarded as bad practice by most players, although in some American schools it might be considered legitimate bluffing.

- Players should not discuss the hand after it is over. It is not good etiquette to spark a post-mortem discussion after the hand has finished – other players are not likely to be interested. In particular, other players' play should not be criticized, nor should 'helpful' advice be offered to other players, who will probably resent it.

- It is in order, in fact desirable, to help the dealer if he makes an error, but not to criticize him.

- Discards should be passed to the dealer in a careful manner, not thrown across the table (especially as this might reveal what they are).

- A player who goes all-in should announce the fact, so that all players, especially the dealer, know the situation. The dealer should announce the fact to all.

- A player going all-in, thus creating a side-pot, must not display his hand until the final showdown. To do so could affect how the players remaining in the side-pot behave.

- When betting, the bet should be clear and not in the nature of a 'feeler'. A player might say 'I bet' or 'I raise' and wait imperceptibly (perhaps fiddling with his chips) for a reaction before deciding how much to bet or raise. Similarly 'I call...' can become '...and raise' according to an opponent's reaction. Bets like this are called 'string bets' and are illegal. Players who do this should be asked to make their bets quicker and clearer.

- When putting chips into the pot a player must be careful that he does it in an orderly way so that all can see the amount. He must not disturb chips already there as this would confuse the picture.

- A player should treat all other players at the table alike. He should not bet more gently against a friend than he would against another.

- It is bad etiquette to take too long to consider one's hand before acting at each betting interval. Some casinos have rules limiting thinking time, say to two minutes, and by agreement this can be applied to private games. It is timed accurately and starts only from when another player requests it, not from some notional idea of how long the player has had.

Should any disputes arise, players should respect the majority opinion.

betting on a certainty

Some friendly poker schools think it is bad etiquette for a player who is holding an unbeatable hand (a royal flush in Draw Poker, or the hole-cards that complete the best possible hand when combined with the board in Hold 'Em or Omaha) to continue to bet. One can see the argument that says one shouldn't take cash from friends by betting on a certainty, but on the other hand if one cannot make a packet on the best hands what is poker about? Nobody is forced to bet against you.

OTHER GAMBLING CARD GAMES

Almost any game, including card games, may be the subject of betting, but some card games are designed wholly for betting. In this section a few of them are described. First are those to be found in casinos: Baccarat and Blackjack; and secondly those played at home: Brag, Napoleon, Red Dog, Rummy, Slippery Sam and Vingt-et-Un.

Baccarat

Baccarat was played for very high stakes by royalty, the aristocracy and rich industrialists, either side of the First World War in French casinos, such as that at Deauville. Nowadays it is found in casinos around the world under different names, often with slight amendments but with the basic rules intact. Described here is a modern version, which might be called Baccarat/*Chemin de Fer* in the United States or *Punto Banco* in the United Kingdom. It is a game of pure chance, with no skill involved.

Baccarat is played on a green baize table that might be marked as shown below. It has positions for a number of players, in this case 12. The game is operated by croupiers on each side of the table (they might be called dealers or callers).

Slot for discarded playing cards

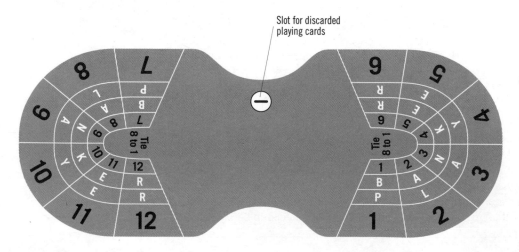

object of the game

The object is to have a hand of a pip count, called a 'point', as near to nine, but not exceeding it, as possible.

- Aces count as one.

- Jacks, Queens and Kings count as ten.

- Only the last digit of the sum of the pips counts. Thus a 7 and a 5, which added together make 12, make a point of 2, a Queen and a 3 make a point of 3, and an Ace and a 6 make a point of 7.

preliminaries

Six or eight packs of cards are shuffled together by the croupiers and placed in a dealing shoe. A marker card is placed between the seventh and eighth card at the back of the shoe to denote the end of the shoe. The hand being played when the marker card appears is played out, but the last few cards remaining are not used.

the play

There are only two hands in Baccarat, the players' and the bank's. So there are only two main available bets:

A Player

B Banker

There is a third bet, a tie, but this is often made as a side-bet, together with one of the others. All players may bet on either player or banker to win by placing their bets (of any size within the casino's limits) in the relevant 'square' in front of them in the section marked 'player' or 'banker'. Bets on a tie go in the small area provided. On some tables the spaces are marked 'Punto' (for player) and 'Banco' (for bank).

All players in rotation are given the chance to play the banker hand, while a croupier plays the player hand. The names 'banker' and 'player', therefore, do not have the usual significance, but this is of no matter, as neither side has any options in its play.

Player 1 has first option to play the banker hand, and thus deal the cards. He is entitled to decline the offer, and the shoe is passed to the next player. It is the action of the shoe passing round the table with each hand like a train that gave the game one of its names, *Chemin de fer*, the French for railway.

1 When the players have made their bets, the player playing banker deals a card face down to the croupier, a card face down to himself, and a second card to each. Initially a hand consists of two cards, although a third might be added later.

2 Both croupier and player look at their hands, and if either has a point of 9 or 8 he exposes the hand immediately. These are 'naturals' and win straightaway, unless of course both the player and banker hands are naturals, when the point of 9 beats the point of 8. Equal hands count as a tie, and all the players retain their stakes.

3 Should no naturals be revealed the hands are returned face down to the table, and the croupier (the player) deals with his own hand first.

   - If his point is 6 or 7 he stands.

   - If it is 0, 1, 2, 3, 4 or 5 he must draw. He asks the player with the shoe, the banker, to give him another card, which is dealt face up.

4 The banker now deals with his hand.

   - If he has a point of 7, he will stand.

   - If the player did not draw, the banker also stands on 6, but draws on 0, 1, 2, 3, 4 or 5.

   - If the player draws, the banker follows the requirements of Table 14.

Player and banker can draw only one card each and no hand can contain more than three cards.

When both hands are completed, they are exposed, the winning hand being that nearer 9 but not exceeding it.

Bets are now settled as follows:

   - If the player wins, his backers are paid at even money.

TABLE 14: Banker's Table of Play in Baccarat/Punto Banco

Banker's point	Must draw if player draws	Must stands if player draws
0, 1, 2	0, 1, 2, 3, 4, 5, 6, 7, 8, 9	
3	0, 1, 2, 3, 4, 5, 6, 7, 9	8
4	2, 3, 4, 5, 6, 7	0, 1, 8, 9
5	4, 5, 6, 7	0, 1, 2, 3, 8, 9
6	6, 7	0, 1, 2, 3, 4, 5, 8, 9

- If the banker wins, the casino pays at odds of 19 to 20, i.e. five per cent less than evens. This is because the Table of Play for the banker, whose hand is dealt with second, is worked out to give him the optimum chance. In fact, it has been calculated that the banker has a 1.34 per cent advantage over the player, so by paying out at 19 to 20, the casino converts that adverse percentage into an edge of 1.20 per cent for itself. Backing bank is a slightly better bet than backing player.

Equal hands are a stand-off and stakes are returned. People who backed tie are paid at odds of 8 to 1, but since the true odds are nearer 19 to 2, the casino gains an advantage of around 14 per cent.

Variant

In the traditional form of Baccarat, and *Chemin de Fer*, the Table of Play for both player and banker gave both the option of drawing or standing on a point of 5, but this affects the game very little.

Blackjack

Blackjack is played at a casino table like that shown below. Usually seven players can be accommodated at the table, with the dealer facing them.

Up to eight packs of cards are used, and are shuffled by the dealer. One player is allowed to cut the cards by inserting an indicator card into the combined pack. The dealer completes the cut and places the pack face down in a dealing shoe, with the indicator card a few cards (up to 50) from the bottom of the pack – these last cards will not be used.

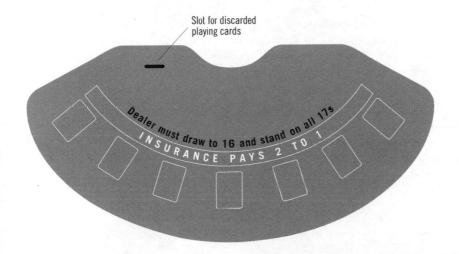

Slot for discarded playing cards

Dealer must draw to 16 and stand on all 17s

INSURANCE PAYS 2 TO 1

the object of the game

The object, from the players' point of view, is to obtain a total card count, with the two cards dealt or with others as well, that is higher than that of the dealer, but not exceeding a maximum of 21. Should a player's count exceed 21 he has *busted* and loses. A count of 21 with two cards (Ace and a ten-count) is a *natural* or *blackjack* and beats any other hand. When a player wins with a blackjack the dealer pays him at odds of 3 to 2 (this is sometimes stated on the table). All other bets are settled at 1 to 1, and all ties are a stand-off and the player retains his stake. When the dealer has a blackjack he wins all stakes, except from a player with a blackjack, in which case the bet is a stand-off.

All cards have their pip value, except:

- King, Queen and Jack count as 10.

- The Ace when held by the player can count one or 10 at his discretion. It also has these values when held by the dealer, but subject to restrictions, as we will see. A hand which counts an Ace as 11 is known as a 'soft' hand (e.g. Ace, 6 is a 'soft 17'). Once the Ace is counted as one it is a 'hard' hand (e.g. Ace, 6, 10 is a 'hard 17').

the play

Before the deal, players put their stakes in the betting space before them, subject to the casino's limits.

The dealer burns the first card from the shoe, then deals one card to each player face up, beginning with the player on his left, and ending with one to himself. He then deals a second card all round, but this time his own card is face down.

If the dealer's face-up card is an Ace, he invites all players to 'insure' against him holding a blackjack. A player who wishes to do so puts up a premium of half his stake. The dealer then looks at his face-down card and if it is a ten-count, declares his blackjack. Players who insured are paid at odds of 2 to 1, and therefore retain their stake and premium, and neither win nor lose on the deal. If the dealer's face-up card is a ten-count, he also looks at his face-down card. Should he have a blackjack he declares it and settles all bets. In this case, insurance does not arise.

When the dealer does not have a blackjack, his face-down card remains face down, so his total count is unknown, and he deals with all players in turn from his left.

Each player has four options.

- If he is satisfied with his count (say, if it is 19 or 20) he will stand.

- He can draw another card, dealt face up. A traditional way of doing this is to say to the dealer, 'Hit me.' He can continue to draw cards until satisfied with his count. If he busts (i.e. exceeds 21) he loses, and the dealer collects his stake.

- If he has two cards of the same rank, he may *split his pairs*. If he does, in effect each card becomes the first card of a separate hand, and the player puts a stake equal to his original stake on the second card. The dealer deals a second card to each card and the player plays each hand in turn. Should the second card in a split hand form another pair, he may split them again.

If a player splits a pair of Aces, he may not draw a third card to either hand. If he receives another Ace, he may split again. A blackjack scored with a split hand wins immediately, but is paid only at 1 to 1, not 3 to 2.

- He can *double down*. This allows him to double his stake and receive a third card face down. This completes his hand, and the card remains face down until the settlement.

the dealer's hand

When the hands of all players who have not bust are complete, the dealer faces his second card to expose his hand. He has no options in playing his hand. If his count is 16 or fewer he must draw and continue until his count is 17, 18, 19, 20 or 21, when he must stand. Should the dealer bust, all the players still in the game win.

The dealer may count an Ace as either one or 11, but only if his total does not reach one of 17–21. As soon as one of those numbers can be made, he must stand. For example, if he holds Ace-6 (a 'soft' 17), he must stand on 17, although if a player held Ace-6, he would do best to draw or double down, according to the dealer's up-card.

When the dealer stands, he pays all players with a count higher than him, and collects the stakes of those with a lower count. Where counts are tied, the player retains his stake.

strategy

As stated above, a player's main choices are whether to stand, hit or double down. Experts have worked out the optimum play and this is shown in Tables 15 and 16 (overleaf).

TABLE 15: Player's optimum play at Blackjack
Hard 2-card total

Player holds	Dealer's face-up card									
	2	3	4	5	6	7	8	9	10	A
17	S	S	S	S	S	S	S	S	S	S
16	S	S	S	S	S	H	H	H	S	S
15	S	S	S	S	S	H	H	H	H	H
14	S	S	S	S	S	H	H	H	H	H
13	S	S	S	S	S	H	H	H	H	H
12	H	H	S	S	S	H	H	H	H	H
11	D	D	D	D	D	D	D	D	D	D
10	D	D	D	D	D	D	D	D	H	H
9	D	D	D	D	D	H	H	H	H	H

TABLE 16: Player's optimum play at Blackjack
Soft 2-card total

Player holds	Dealer's face-up card									
	2	3	4	5	6	7	8	9	10	A
19	S	S	S	S	S	S	S	S	S	S
18	S	S	S	S	S	S	H	H	H	H
17	D	D	D	D	D	H	H	H	H	H
16	H	H	H	H	D	H	H	H	H	H
15	H	H	H	H	D	H	H	H	H	H
14	H	H	H	H	D	H	H	H	H	H
13	H	H	H	H	D	H	H	H	H	H

S = stand   H = hit   D = double down

Always stand on hard hands of 17 or more and soft hands of 19 and 20.

The other choice involves whether or not to split pairs. Again experts have worked out the optimum play, and this is shown in Table 17.

TABLE 17: Advisability of splitting pairs

Player holds	Dealer's face-up card									
	2	3	4	5	6	7	8	9	10	A
A	S	S	S	S	S	S	S	S	S	S
10	X	X	X	X	X	X	X	X	X	X
9	S	S	S	S	S	X	X	X	X	X
8	S	S	S	S	S	S	S	X	X	S
7	S	S	S	S	S	S	X	X	X	X
6	S	S	S	S	S	X	X	X	X	X
5	X	X	X	X	X	X	X	X	X	X
4	X	X	X	X	X	X	X	X	X	X
3	S	S	S	S	S	S	X	X	X	X
2	S	S	S	S	S	S	X	X	X	X

S = split   X = do not split

insurance

It is not a good idea to take insurance. It is really a side-bet offering odds of 2 to1 for what is really a 9 to 4 chance. Although the player appears to have the advantage, in that he has all the options and receives the bonus payment for blackjacks, the casino, of course, wouldn't offer the game if it did not have an edge. The edge comes from the fact that the player plays first, and always loses if he busts. When the dealer busts, he loses only to those hands still active. If four players have busted already, the dealer who busts loses to the other three but still wins from four – thus it is not strictly true to say that ties are a stand-off. However, a player who makes the right options will find the casino edge very small, not more than one per cent.

variants

Some casinos will have variations on the above, such as any of the following:

- The dealer will draw on soft 17 (the rule should be printed on the table).

- The casino will not offer insurance.

- The players' cards will be dealt face down.

- Doubling down will be restricted to certain hands (usually 9, 10 or 11).

- Splitting pairs might be restricted.

Most of these are harmless and will not seriously affect the players' chances. However, one variation, known as the 'London deal', does affect the players' chances. It entails the dealer not dealing his second card until after the players have bet. This was originally meant to prevent the possibility of cheating by collusion between dealer and player, but means players might increase their stakes only to find the dealer ultimately holds a blackjack. If this is in operation, it is best not to double down, to split only Aces, and to bet conservatively when dealer's first card is an Ace or a 10-count card.

Brag

Edmond Hoyle, who died in 1769 aged nearly 100, wrote about Brag, although he had never heard of 99 per cent of the games whose rules are set out in modern 'Hoyles'. Brag is an ancestor of poker, and many textbooks still describe 'classical' Brag, although it is a game practically never played these days. However, many modern versions of Brag are played. The following version is perhaps the most popular.

The game is for three or more players, perhaps about six being the best number. The standard pack of 52 cards is used, the cards generally ranking from Ace (high) to 2, but with exceptions as detailed in the ranking of hands, given opposite. The object of the game is to win the pot by having the best hand remaining at the showdown. There are six classes of hand, as shown opposite.

HIGHEST   **LOWEST**

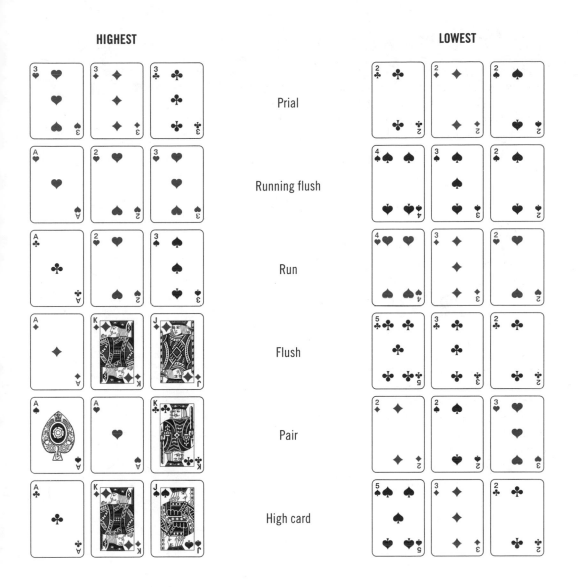

Prial

Running flush

Run

Flush

Pair

High card

The ranking of hands within each class, and the probabilities of each class of hand, are shown in Table 18 overleaf.

TABLE 18: The ranking of Brag hands

		Combinations	Probability	Description
Prial		52	0.24%	Three cards of the same rank. Among prials, the highest is usually regarded as a prial of 3s, after that a prial of Aces down to a prial of 2s.
Running flush		48	0.22%	Three cards in sequence of the same suit. Ace can count high or low, thus A, K, Q is a sequence, as is 3, 2, A. So far as sequences rank, A, 2, 3 is the highest, followed by A, K, Q, then K, Q, J down to 4, 3, 2.
Run		720	3.26%	Three cards in sequence. Again A, 2, 3 ranks highest, followed by A, K, Q down to 4, 3, 2.
Flush		1,096	4.96%	Three cards of the same suit. Within flushes that with the highest-ranking card wins (Ace being high), if equal second highest, if again equal third.
Pair		3,744	16.94%	One pair with an odd card. Within pairs the highest-ranking pair wins (Aces high), if equal the odd card decides.
High card		16,440	74.39%	None of the above combinations, i.e. three cards of differing ranks not of the same suit. The highest card (Ace high) determines the best hand, if equal the second, etc.

ranking of Brag Hands

The Brag hands, with the number of possible such hands, and the percentage probability of being dealt them, are shown in Table 18. It will be seen there is an anomaly here, in that a running flush is slightly harder to get than a prial, although it is ranked lower. Over 90 per cent of hands produce no better than a pair.

preliminaries

Brag is a staking game and a minimum and maximum stake should be agreed beforehand. The maximum stake is not the maximum for a single bet or raise, but the maximum a player may bet on one hand. The length of time for the game should be agreed, and once the time is up the game should end as soon as all players have dealt an equal number of hands. It is also a game where some schools prefer the cards to be shuffled between each deal and others not. A compromise is to agree a light shuffle.

dealing

Players cut the cards to determine first dealer, the holder of the highest card dealing. Dealer shuffles and the player to his right cuts. After each hand the deal passes to the left. Whatever has been agreed about shuffling, the cards should be cut before each deal. Before dealing, the dealer puts in the pot an initial stake between the agreed limits. He then deals the cards one at a time to each player, including himself, starting on his left and ending when all players have three cards.

betting and showdown

As stated, the dealer has put a stake into the pot. Beginning with the player to his left, and in rotation, each player, including the dealer, must do one of the following:

- Put in a stake equal to the dealer's.

- Raise the stake by equalling the dealer's stake and adding an extra stake, without exceeding the maximum agreed stake.

- Throw in his hand.

Once the stake has been raised, following players must equal it or raise it, and when the turn comes round to those who have already staked, they must equal or increase the stake, too. Unlike in poker, the betting does not necessarily stop once all players' stakes are equal, because the last raiser may raise again, provided the maximum stake for a hand has not been reached.

The betting ends only when one of the following occurs:

- All players but one have folded (when the remaining one takes the pot).

- The stakes of all who remain in are equal and the last raiser does not wish to raise again.

- The agreed maximum stake the players may bet on one hand has been reached.

If there is a showdown, the player with the best Brag hand wins the pot – if hands are tied, the pot is shared equally.

variants

Some schools do not admit a prial of 3s as the best hand, but rank prials from Aces (high) to 2s (low). In addition, some schools do not allow a run of A, 2, 3 to beat A, K, Q. Instead of being the highest run, A, 2, 3 becomes the lowest.

Seven-card Brag

There are two versions of Seven-card Brag:

A Players are dealt seven cards each from which they select their best three-card Brag hand, discarding face down the remaining four cards. The betting then proceeds as in the parent game.

B Players each put an agreed stake into a pot. There is no conventional betting. They then arrange their seven cards into two hands, discarding the odd card face down. The two hands are also placed face down. When all are ready, each reveals his better hand. When the best hand is determined, all players reveal their second hand. If the same player has the best hand in each case, he scoops the pot. Otherwise the pot remains for the next hand, to which all contribute a second stake. Thus with each deal which passes without a winner, the pot increases in size.

A player is not obliged to make his first hand the best possible. For example, suppose his seven cards were as in the hand shown opposite. His best hand would be a prial of Aces, practically certain to win, with the second hand King high, almost certain not to. His best bet, however, would be to make his first hand ◆A, ◆K, ◆Q and his second ♥A, ♥2, ♣3, discarding the third Ace. This would give him an excellent chance of the pot. Each player's first hand should remain exposed while the second hands are examined, to ensure the hands are played in the correct order.

Nine-card Brag

This is played in a similar way to Seven-card Brag. Nine cards are dealt to each player, who makes three hands. A player winning all three takes the pot; otherwise the pot is strengthened and the deal passes to the next player. The pot can get very large before somebody wins it.

Napoleon

Napoleon, usually called Nap, is for two to eight players (it works best with about five), played with the standard pack of cards, which rank from Ace high to 2 low. The object for the declarer is to make the number of *tricks* he contracted for, and his opponents' object is to prevent him.

Cards are cut for first dealer, after which the deal passes to the left.

the play

The dealer deals five cards to each player, one at a time. There is then a single bidding round, in which each player, beginning with the one on dealer's left, has one chance only to bid or pass. A *bid* is a contract to make a given number of tricks. The lowest bid is two, and the highest – five – is called 'nap'. If all players pass, the dealer, as last to speak, is permitted to bid one. Any bid must be higher than a previous bid.

The highest bidder becomes the *declarer* and he *leads* to the first trick, the suit of the card led being the trump suit. Players from his left play a card each to complete the trick. The usual rules of trick-taking games apply:

- Players must follow suit to the card led if able, otherwise they may play a trump or discard.

- A trick is won by the highest trump it contains, or if none by the highest card in the suit led.

settlement

Settlement is made at the end of each deal. The declarer receives money from the other players if he makes his contract, but pays them if he does not.

- If successful, the declarer is paid one unit of cash by each player for each trick he contracted for; if he fails, he pays each player on the same scale. *Overtricks* or *undertricks* are of no significance: he either makes the contract or not.

- If the declarer goes nap, and takes all five tricks, he wins ten units of cash from each player: if he fails, he pays them five only.

variants

Some schools allow additional bids. If during the bidding a player bids napoleon, or nap, a subsequent bidder may overbid with a bid of 'wellington', which is also a contract to make all five tricks (it can happen, as the declarer chooses his own trump suit). Another player could then overbid with 'blucher', which outbids wellington (Napoleon, Wellington and Blucher were the three principal commanders at the Battle of Waterloo, but the game was unknown until about 60 years later). Wellington can be bid only after a bid of napoleon, and blucher only after wellington. Wellington and blucher, like nap, win ten units if successful, but if unsuccessful, the declarer pays each player ten units for wellington and 20 for blucher.

Some schools allow a further bid of 'misère' or 'misery', an undertaking to lose all five tricks. It ranks between bids of three and four, and is paid out at three units per player. Usually it is played without trumps, but some schools prefer the first card led (as before, by the bidder) to denote a trump suit.

Red Dog

Red Dog is a simple gambling game of little skill – really a social game for enjoyment rather than serious betting. It is best played if the dealer takes no part – as the deal passes quickly round the table it is worth the inconvenience of not playing for a couple of minutes.

Up to ten players can play and they bet against a pool rather than a banker or each other, and all must contribute equally to the pool. If there are ten players, each might contribute two or three units to the pool; if only three or four, perhaps five or six units.

the play

1 The first dealer is chosen by any convenient method and, after shuffling and a cut by the player on his right, he deals five cards to each player, excluding himself, face down (if there are between eight and ten players, four cards each would be better). The dealer places the remaining cards face down before him to form a stock.

2 The player on the dealer's left looks at his cards and bets any amount from one unit to the entire amount in the pool that he has a card to beat the top card of the stock. To beat it he must hold a card of higher rank in the same suit. To make his bet the player pushes his stake towards the pool.

3 Once the bet is made, dealer faces the top card of the stock.

4 If the player has a card to beat it, he exposes it. The dealer then adds an equal amount from the pool to the player's stake and the player withdraws it. His cards, and the top card of the stock, are collected up and go face down onto a discard pile. The other players do not see his unused cards.

   If the player cannot beat the card exposed, his stake is added to the pool. He must expose his whole hand face up so that the other players can note the cards he held and then his hand is collected up and discarded face down.

   If his hand is so poor that he is unlikely to beat any card, a player may pay one unit to the pool instead of betting, and his cards are discarded unseen by other players. A player cannot gain from this, but some think it worthwhile as it prevents the others knowing which cards were in his hand, which they would do if he bet and lost.

5 Then it is the next player's turn.

6 Once all of the active players have had their turn, the deal passes to the player on the first dealer's left, who shuffles and cuts again.

---

filling the pool

If at any time the pool disappears by virtue of a player winning it, all players must contribute equally as before to form a new pool of the same amount.

If at the changeover of dealer the pool has become low (say no more than one chip per player) then the pool should be replenished by all contributing the same number of chips again.

variants

Some schools allow a player to bet that he cannot beat the top card. If he bets that he will lose, his entire hand must be exposed before it is discarded, whether he wins or not.

As players need hold no more than two Aces, or perhaps a card higher than 8 in each suit, to have a better than even chance of beating the dealer's up-card, the pool gets taken regularly and players find it tedious to continually replenish it. A betting limit can therefore be imposed: players can bet, say, up to five units only. This cuts down the number of times the pool needs replenishing.

Rummy

Rummy is really a whole family of card games, which have proliferated in the last 150 years or so, possibly from the old Mexican game of Conquian.

A popular version is described here, suitable for from three to six players (two players might prefer Gin Rummy, which follows). The standard pack of 52 cards is used, ranking from King (high) to Ace (low). The players draw cards to pick the first dealer – lowest deals. He shuffles and the player to his right cuts.

the object of the game

Each player's object is to get rid of all the cards in his hand by laying down sets *(melds)* of either:

● three or four cards of the same rank.

● sequences of three or more cards of the same suit.

the play

1 With three or four players, the dealer deals seven cards one at a time to each player, including himself (with five or six players, he deals six cards each). The remainder of the pack is placed face down on the table to form the stock, and the top card is turned face up and placed beside the stock to begin a discard pile.

2 Each player in turn, beginning on dealer's left, draws a card either from the top of the discard pile, or from the top of the stock. If he draws from the stock, he does not disclose the card to other players.

3 At this point he can lay down in front of him any melds he has in his hand, and can add a card or cards to an existing meld of his own, or *lay off* cards on to melds of other players. He can do any or all of these things on the same turn.

4 He then discards a card from his hand to the discard pile. He may discard the card that he drew if it is of no use to him.

The first player thus to get rid of all his cards wins the hand. On his last turn, if he wishes, he can meld all the cards in his hand without making the usual discard.

Should the stock become exhausted before a player has gone out, the discard pile is turned over to become the stock, play continuing as usual.

Settlement

When one player has gone out the other players are debited with all the unmelded cards left in their hands, on the following count:

- court cards (K, Q, J) – ten points.
- all other cards – pip value.
- Aces – one point.

Settlement is made after each hand at the rate of one unit of cash per point, or if preferred one per ten points, with the total rounded up to the nearest ten.

Gin Rummy

This is the best-known variant of Rummy, and is designed for two players. The players draw to decide the first dealer, the player with the higher card having the choice of whether to deal or not. The dealer shuffles and the non-dealer cuts. Like the parent game, the object is to get rid of cards by forming sets. Unlike in the parent game, however, the sets are held in the hand until the end of the game.

the play

1 The dealer deals ten cards one at a time to both players, beginning with the non-dealer. The remainder of the pack is placed face down to form the stock, and the top card is turned face up beside it to become the first up-card, on what will become a discard pile.

2 The non-dealer may take the first up-card into his hand or refuse it. If he takes it he replaces it with a discard from his hand. If he refuses it, it is the dealer's turn and he has the same options.

3 If both players refuse the up-card, the non-dealer takes the top card of the stock into his hand and discards a card (it might be the same one if he doesn't want it) by placing it face up on the up-card, which becomes now a discard pile. From now on each player may take either the discard or the top card of the stock into his hand. He then discards to keep ten cards in his hand. Players may not look back through the discards unless this has been agreed beforehand.

4 Both players continue to pick up and discard until one of them has enough sets to go out.

going out

When a player has all the sets he can, he may be left with a few unmatched cards. After drawing a card from the stock or discard pile he may go out (knock) if the unmatched cards in his hand (not counting the discard) count ten points or fewer (scoring is the same as in the main game).

To knock, a player lays down his ten cards arranged in sets with any unmatched cards to one side. The left-hand layout opposite, shows such an arrangement. The player has three sets and his unmatched card counts two. He is said to 'knock for two'.

- If a player lays down all his cards without any unmatched cards, he is said to go gin.

- If the fiftieth card is drawn from stock, leaving only two, and the drawer discards without knocking, the opposing player may pick up the discard and knock, but may not draw from stock. The last two cards remain unplayed. If this player also does not knock, the deal is abandoned, and the player who dealt deals again.

laying off

When one player knocks, his opponent also lays down the cards in his own hand. If any of his unmatched cards fit in with the knocker's sets he may lay them off, reducing the count against himself.

For example, suppose he lays down the cards in the layout, opposite right, his opponent having knocked with the other hand. His unmatched cards are ♠9, ♦9, ♠A for a count of 19. However, he can lay off ♠9 at the top end of knocker's ♠8, ♠7, ♠6 and his ♦9 on knocker's ♦Q, ♦J, ♦10. His count is reduced to 1.

Going out

Laying off

However, it is not possible to lay off cards on a knocker who goes gin. If the unmatched ♣2 in the hand of the knocker (above left) had been a 4, say, the knocker could have added it to his set of 4s and gone gin, not allowing any cards to be laid off on him.

scoring

- If the knocker has the lower count of unmatched cards in the two hands, he scores the difference in the two counts.

- If, however, the opponent's count is equal to or lower than the knocker's, he is said to have *undercut* the knocker. He then scores the difference, if any, between the two counts plus a bonus of 25 points for undercutting. Thus the knocker above is unlucky, as his opponent, by laying off and reducing his count to 1, has undercut him. He thereby scores 1, plus the bonus of 25, making 26 points.

- When the knocker goes gin, he cannot be undercut, as his opponent cannot lay off any unmatched cards. He scores the difference in the count plus a bonus of 25 for going gin.

The score for each player is entered on a score sheet:

- The first player to score 100 points wins the game.

- For each hand a player wins within the game he scores 25 points.

- The winner gets an additional bonus of 100 points.

- If the loser did not score a single point, the winner's total is doubled.

The payout is at a rate agreed beforehand, perhaps one unit of cash per point, or per ten or 20 points.

Slippery Sam

Slippery Sam, also called Shoot, is a banking game that is rare in that it favours the players over the bank. Indeed the banker is likely to lose all his money. It is a very similar game to Red Dog.

Any number from three to about ten may play, with about six people the best. The standard pack is used, cards ranking from Ace (high) to 2 (low).

Players draw cards to decide who is first banker, the highest being first dealer. It is necessary to agree beforehand that all the players should hold the bank an equal number of times, as the banker will almost certainly lose. For the same reason a standard amount for the bank should be agreed. It is best also to agree a minimum bet.

The banker puts the agreed amount into the centre as the bank. He has the right to shuffle last and the player on his right cuts.

the play

1 The banker deals three cards, one at a time, to each player (but not himself), beginning on his left, and places the remaining cards face down before him to become the stock.

2 The player on the banker's left examines his cards and bets any amount between the agreed minimum and the total of the bank that he will beat the top card of the stock. To do so he must hold a card of the same suit but higher in rank.

3 When he has made his bet the banker exposes the top card of the stock. If the player has a card to beat it he shows it and is paid by the banker the amount of his stake. It he hasn't, he adds the amount of his stake to the bank without exposing his cards. The four cards (banker's and player's) are collected by the banker and put aside face down.

4   While any money remains in the bank, each player goes in turn. No player may look at his cards until it is his turn to bet.

5   If the whole bank is taken, that banker's turn is ended, and the bank passes to the next player on the left, who puts in the agreed amount. Otherwise the banker holds the bank for three rounds, the cards being shuffled and cut between each round. If anything remains in the bank after three rounds, the banker may, if he wishes, hold the bank for one more round only. Otherwise, and this is his best option, he takes what remains in the bank and passes the cards to the next player.

Vingt-et-Un (Pontoon)

Vingt-et-Un, or Twenty-One, corrupted in English by stages through Van John to Pontoon, is the domestic version of the casino game of Blackjack, and a more varied and interesting game. It is widely played and a game that more than most has local rules. The following version is considered as good as any.

Each player's object is to build a hand with a pip total nearer to 21, but without exceeding it, than the dealer can achieve. An Ace counts 11 or one at the holder's discretion, a court card (K, Q, J) 10, and other cards at their pip value. About five to eight players is best. The standard pack of 52 cards is used.

The traditional way to choose first banker is for one player to shuffle the cards and deal them face up one at a time to each player until a Jack appears to denote the first dealer. He shuffles and the player to his right cuts.

the play

1   The dealer is in effect a banker, who plays against the players. He deals one card face down to each player, and to himself. The players look at their cards and stake any amount they wish between an agreed minimum and maximum (a maximum of something like six to ten times the minimum is recommended).

2   The players state their stakes and place them on the table.

3   The banker deals another card face down to all players, and to himself.

4   The players look at their cards and if any of them holds an Ace and a ten-count (a pontoon) exposes it. This is the highest hand and can only be beaten if the dealer also has one.

5 The dealer deals with each player in turn, beginning with the one on his left.

6 A player has three choices when the dealer comes to deal with his hand. He can:

- **Stand** (stick) He takes no more cards, being happy with his total. He may not stand if his total is 15 or fewer (unless he has five cards, as will be seen).

- **Buy** He may buy a further card face down, for a stake not exceeding his original stake. He may buy further cards in the same way, but his hand must not exceed five cards, which is a maximum hand. He cannot buy a fifth card if his four-card total is 11 or lower, but may twist.

- **Twist** He asks the dealer to twist him a further card face up, for which he does not pay. A player may twist at any time, even if he has previously bought cards.

If during play, a player's count, either on buying a card or twisting, exceeds 21, he busts and throws in his hand. The dealer puts his cards on the bottom of the pack and collects the bust player's stake.

7 When all players have been dealt with, the banker exposes his own two cards. If he holds a pontoon, he collects all the stakes, including those of any player with a pontoon. Otherwise, he may stand, or deal himself extra cards, standing when he wishes. He can count Ace as 11 or one and, apart from being unable to split Aces, has no restrictions at all. Should his count exceed 21, however, he loses to all the players still in the game.

the five-card hand

Another special hand, in addition to the pontoon mentioned above, is the five-card hand, i.e. a hand containing five cards whose pip count does not exceed 21. This hand beats all others, irrespective of count, except a pontoon.

settlement

When the dealer stands, settlement is made in the following way:

- He pays all players whose totals are nearer 21, and collects from those whose totals are equal or lower.

- Unless he holds a five-card hand he pays all five-card hands. If he holds a five-card hand he collects from holders of five-card hands.

- A player who holds pontoon is paid double by the dealer, but players do not pay double to a dealer with a pontoon.

the next deal

After each deal the cards are shuffled and cut. The deal does not pass on by rotation; the dealer retains the bank until a player holds a pontoon, when that player takes it for the next deal. The only exceptions to this are if the pontoon was from split Aces or the dealer also holds a pontoon, when the dealer retains the bank. Should two or more players hold a pontoon on the same hand, the player nearest the dealer's left takes over the bank.

Although players have the advantage of determining their stakes, the advantage is with the bank, which is usually profitable, because the dealer wins on tied hands, and because he wins from all players who bust, even though he might eventually bust himself.

split Aces

A player who has been dealt a pair of Aces may split them. He separates the cards and places the same stake as his original stake on the second card. Each card is now regarded as the first card of separate hands and is dealt with separately. If a third Ace is dealt on either of the two Aces it can also be split.

GLOSSARY

Where no game is mentioned, the terms relate to poker.

Aces up Two pairs, the higher being Aces. Also Kings up, etc.

All-in To have all one's chips in the pot.

Ante A compulsory stake made before the deal.

Back door (Hold 'Em and Omaha) To complete a flush or straight with the last two board cards, when this was not the primary objective.

Betting intervals The periods in a deal when players must bet, raise, call, check or fold.

Blind Compulsory bets made by the first two players to the left of dealer before the deal. The first is a 'small blind', and the second, usually of twice or three times the amount, a 'big blind'. They count as active bets.

Board The set of communal cards turned up on the table.

Bug A single wild card, usually the Joker.

Burn To remove from play the first down-card before dealing (to prevent cheating).

Bust (Blackjack and Pontoon) To reach a total of over 21.

Call To match the previous bet.

Case card The fourth card of a rank, when the other three are already in play.

Cash in To cash one's chips and retire from the game.

Check To stay in the game without betting. Sometimes indicated by tapping the table (but all must agree this convention). A player who checks may later bet or call.

Chips The counters of various colours used to bet with, each colour representing a different amount of money.

Community cards Those cards in games like Hold 'Em which are common to all players' hands.

Declarer (Napoleon) The highest bidder who plays against all other players.

Deuce A card of the 2 rank.

Double Down (Blackjack) To double the stake on a hand and receive a third card.

Draw The exchange of some cards in a poker hand for others.

Fifth street The fifth and final community card in Hold 'Em and Omaha. Also known as the river.

Flop The first three community cards in Hold 'Em and Omaha.

Flush Five cards of the same suit.

Fold To take no further part in a deal.

Fourth street The fourth community card in Hold 'Em and Omaha. Also known as the turn.

Freeze-out A game in which all players start with equal chips and play until one player has won all the chips.

Full house Three cards of the same rank and two of a different rank.

Go gin (Gin Rummy) To go out without any unmatched cards.

Go out (Gin Rummy) To lay down one's hand. (Rummy) To get rid of all one's cards.

Hand (a) The five cards that form a player's holding. (b) The action from deal to showdown.

Hard hand (Blackjack) A hand which counts the Ace as one.

Heads up A hand in which only two players remain in the action.

Hole-cards Concealed cards. A player's first card in Stud, first two in Hold 'Em and first four in Omaha.

Inside straight A holding such as 8, 7, 6, 4 that requires a card to fill a gap to make a straight.

Kicker (a) A card retained with a pair at the draw in Draw Poker, e.g. the Ace in A, 10, 10. (b) The lower of the two hole-cards in Hold 'Em, e.g. the 8 in A, 8.

Knocker (Gin Rummy) The player who goes out.

Limits The minimum and maximum amount or number of chips a player is allowed to bet.

Loose player A player who bets in defiance of the odds.

Main pot If a side-pot (q.v.) is formed by a player going all-in (q.v.) the original pot is called the main pot.

Meld (Rummy and Gin Rummy) A set of three or more cards (a) of the same rank (b) of the same suit and in sequence.

Nap (Napoleon) A bid to make all five tricks.

Natural (Baccarat) A point of 8 or 9. (Blackjack) a count of 21 with two cards, an Ace and 10-count.

No-limit A game in which players may bet as many chips as they have on the table. See also 'Table stakes'.

Off-suit Cards of differing suits, particularly in describing the two hole-cards in Hold 'Em.

Open-ended straight A holding such as 8, 7, 6, 5, where a card at either end (9 or 4) will complete a straight.

Openers The cards required to open the betting, e.g. a pair of Jacks in Jackpots.

Pass To fold. In the USA it can also mean to check.

Pat hand A hand in Draw Poker to which no cards need be drawn.

Point (Baccarat) The pip-count of a hand.

Pontoon (Vingt-et-Un) (a) The common English name for vingt-et-un. (b) a count of 21 with two cards, an Ace and 10-count.

Pool (Red Dog) The amount in the centre of the table which players add to or take from.

Position Place at the table in relation to dealer; place in the betting order.

Pot The chips or money at stake on the table.

Pot limit A game in which the maximum raise is the total in the pot at the time of betting.

Prial (Brag) A hand of three of a kind.

Quads Four of a kind; four cards of the same rank.

Raise To call and increase the previous bet.

River The last community card on the board.

Round of betting A betting interval.

Royal flush The highest hand in Poker, the A, K, Q, J, 10 of the same suit.

Run A straight.

See To call.

Semi-bluff To bet with a hand not worth much, but with the potential to improve.

Showdown The display of cards at the end of a hand to determine the winner.

Side-pot A separate pot contested by the other players when one player is all-in.

Slow play To bet small or check with a good hand in order to entice others to bet and enlarge the pot.

Soft hand (Blackjack) A hand which counts the Ace as 11.

Split Aces (Vingt-et-Un) To use a pair of Aces as the first cards of two separate hands.

Split pairs (Blackjack) To use a pair as the first cards of two separate hands.

Split pot A pot that is shared because hands are equal.

Stand (Blackjack and Vingt-et-Un) To play with the cards dealt and not buy or twist another.

Stand pat To decline to exchange cards at the draw.

Stay To remain in a pot by calling.

Straddle The last blind before the deal.

Straight Five unsuited cards of consecutive rank.

Straight flush Five cards of consecutive rank and of the same suit.

Table stakes A game in which a player's bet is limited to the amount of money or chips he has on the table before him. No-limit and pot-limit games are played this way.

Tap out To bet all one's chips.

Tight player A player who bets only on strong hands.

Trey A card of the 3 rank.

Trips, triple, triplets Three of a kind, three cards of the same rank.

Turn The fourth communal card at Hold 'Em or Omaha, also called fourth street.

Twist (Vingt-et-Un) To take an extra face-up card.

Undercut (Gin Rummy) To win a hand by having a lower count than the knocker.

Wild card A card that by agreement can represent any other card in the pack.

INDEX

Acknowledgements

Executive Editor Trevor Davis
Editor Jessica Cowie
Design Manager Tokiko Morishima
Design and Illustrations Peter Gerrish
Senior Production Controller Jo Sim